The Economies
of the Soviet Bloc

*A Study of Decision Making
and Resource Allocation*

Stanisław Wellisz

McGraw-Hill Book Company

New York   San Francisco   Toronto   London

c

212784

E cons.

The Economies of the Soviet Bloc

Preface

This study is a primer of soviet-type economics for the Western reader. It is designated for those who do not wish to acquire specialized knowledge, yet who would like to know about the role of consumers and of workers, about the role of the Communist Party leadership and planners, and about planning objectives and methods behind the Iron Curtain.

The study aims to show in a broad and general way how the system works, and to analyze how economic decisions are reached and how they are put into practice. Historical descriptions and comparisons with free-enterprise economies are kept to a minimum; they are used only to make the analysis intelligible.

By a soviet-type economy I mean the system which prevails in Russia and in the other Communist-controlled countries of Eastern Europe. Each of these countries has certain idiosyncrasies, and no two are identical. Yet just as it is legitimate to talk about free-enterprise economies, so it is possible to talk about the soviet-type economies as a group. Illustrations of the working of the market may be drawn from American, French, or Italian experience; in each case institutional details vary, but the analytical framework is the same. The same holds true of the Soviet-bloc countries. Beneath the surface differences there is an underlying sameness of economic structures.

The main body of Marxian thought explaining and justifying the institutions and policies of the Soviet economies has originated in the Soviet Union. Most of the quotations giving a Marxian explanation of the system are taken, therefore, from Russian sources. Illustrations showing how this type of economy functions are largely though not exclusively based on Polish experience, since of all the countries of the Soviet bloc Poland relies least on official secrecy to shroud the operations of its economy. Every effort was made, however, to illustrate the general principles of the system and to avoid discussion of peculiarities of the Polish economy, and frequent references are made to the experience of other countries in the Soviet sphere.

Where I have quoted from Polish and Russian sources, the translations are mine unless there is a note to the contrary.

In the preparation of this study I have greatly benefited from the cooperation and advice of the Polish Central Planning Commission. I also wish to thank the members of the economics faculties of Warsaw University and of the Central School of Planning and Statistics. Since my conclusions are likely to clash with the views of those who were of most help to me, I want to thank them collectively while disassociating them from my results.

Stanisław Wellisz

Contents

1

Scope and Method
of the Study

The Soviet Union and the countries lying in the Soviet orbit have developed in the last forty years an economic system vastly different from the system of the capitalistic West. While in the West the means of production are in private hands, in Soviet-bloc countries most of the productive power belongs to the state. In the West the economy is "free"; in the Soviet-bloc countries it is "planned." These are the most obvious differences, but they are not the most important ones. There are Western countries, such as France or Italy, in which the nationalization of the means of production is far advanced. Government planning is also a part of the Western economic system; the Netherlands, for instance, attempts to control employment, wages, and the foreign balance through policy tools much more refined than those

available to the Soviet planners. Italy plans the industrialization of its Southern provinces. Even the United States, the
freest of the free enterprise countries, plans through its Federal Reserve and Treasury policy.

Where, then, lies the chief difference between Western
and soviet-type economies? It lies in the role assigned to
the market. In the West the principal decisions of the economic system are made with reference to the market situation and are carried out through the market mechanism. In
the soviet-type economies the principal decisions ignore the
market, and the market plays little or no role in the transmission of orders or the collection of information. Thus the
soviet-type economies had to develop channels of communication and control which do not exist and which are
not necessary in the West.

The reliance or nonreliance on the market mechanism
clarifies the qualitative difference between Western and
Soviet planning. Planning in the West consists essentially
of modifying the functioning, or in some cases, the structure, of the market. The Federal Reserve interferes in the
money market by changing reserve and margin requirements and by open-market operations. The Italian government interferes with the factor market by giving subsidies
to enterprises locating in the South. Even government-built
projects operate, albeit sometimes with heavy subsidies, by
selling on the market. In some cases, the market mechanism
is modified, for instance through maximum or minimum
pricing, but only in exceptional cases (as in wartime) is
there any attempt to construct an administrative distribution
mechanism.

In the soviet-type economies, by contrast, the market

plays a peripheral role. Free markets are tolerated as a transitional phenomenon because planners are as yet incapable of being (and, indeed, unwilling to be) concerned with all the minutiae of consumer needs. Consequently some agricultural commodities (mainly fruit, eggs, and vegetables) are not controlled. There are also privately produced services and goods bought and sold on markets of diverse shades of illegality. Finally, there is the black market, a significant pathological manifestation of malfunctioning of planning, but improved methods of planning and control gradually put it out of existence.

Allocation of consumers' goods and of labor may seem at first glance to follow market rules, since consumers choose their purchase patterns and workers choose their own jobs. In reality, these are not genuine markets. Consumers' purchases have no direct effect on the production of consumers' goods, nor workers' choices on the demand for workers. In one case the supply and in the other the demand is administratively determined.

The difference between a market economy and a nonmarket one necessitates the reexamination of all concepts familiar in Western economics and makes all comparisons of the two systems extremely difficult. In the West the concepts of national income and national product refer to the growth of the basket of goods produced for, or purchased on, the national market. In the ultimate analysis we attempt to measure the satisfaction of consumers' wants or the economic potential to satisfy these wants. In the soviet-type economies, on the other hand, national income is the measure of satisfaction of the policy makers' wishes. In one case the product is evaluated by the market, in the

other, by the political leaders. We can, of course, devise a
link between the two concepts and consider the potential of
a soviet-type economy to produce a free-enterprise product
mix, and vice versa. Yet the fact remains that if we are to
use national income as a measure of actual achievement
and not as a measure of potential, we must measure each
system in terms of accomplishment of vastly different goals.

Similar difficulties arise in comparing the "efficiency" of
the two systems. In the West we measure efficiency by
comparing actual performance with the performance of a
hypothetical perfect market. A system is inefficient, if, by
instituting the perfect market, we could satisfy some wants
more fully without lessening the satisfaction of any wants.
The method of measurement is dangerous, because we
make the assumption (and this assumption is not necessarily correct) that such an ideal system could in fact be
devised. In measuring the efficiency of the soviet-type systems, the assumption that a free-market mechanism could
achieve the same results seems completely unwarranted, especially if among "results" we include social goals. One may
wonder, for instance, if any free-market mechanism could
achieve the rate of accumulation now existing in the "popular democracies" of Eastern Europe, or urbanize a country
as fast as the Communist regime urbanized Poland. If the
rate of accumulation or the rate of urbanization is the
planners' goal, then the only valid comparison of efficiency
is with some system, real or hypothetical, which would also
achieve this goal.[1]

[1] For a discussion of the difficulties encountered in comparing the performance of the American economy with that of the
Soviet Union, see Robert W. Campbell, "Problems of United

Despite the difficulties, comparisons of the achievements of free enterprise and of the soviet-type systems are of great interest. There is much concern both here and among the so-called "uncommitted nations" in the relative performance of Russia and the United States or of China and India. Painstaking work by American economists has resulted in a number of studies which, despite inevitable shortcomings, give sound basis for interesting comparisons.[2] Comparisons of the performance of the two systems are also frequently made in the Soviet-bloc countries, as witnessed by numerous publications.[3]

Another line of inquiry on the functioning of soviet-type systems concentrates on the institutional side. Such inquiries permit us to understand the Soviet system by showing the contrasts as well as the parallels with free-enterprise institutions. Banking may serve here as an example. Banks in the free-enterprise economies play an important role in the financial market: They gather financial resources and allocate them (more or less correctly) in accordance with market demands. In the soviet-type economies the finan-

States–Soviet Economic Comparisons," in Joint Economic Committee, Congress of the United States, *Comparisons of the United States and Soviet Economies,* United States Government Printing Office, 1960, part 1, pp. 13–30.

[2] See Abram Bergson, *The Real National Income of Soviet Russia since 1928,* Cambridge, Mass., Harvard University Press, 1961. A very sceptical appraisal of Soviet Russia's achievements will be found in G. Warren Nutter, "The Structure and Growth of Soviet Industry: A Comparison with the United States," Joint Economic Committee, *op. cit.,* pp. 95–120.

[3] See, for instance, A. Alexieiev (ed.), *Ekonomicheskoe Sorevnovanie miezhdu SSSR i SSA,* Moskva, Gosplanizdat, 1959.

cial role of banks is largely passive since the government is the sole source of finance and investments proceed according to plan. Soviet banks have an active role in the control of industry, which their free-enterprise counterparts lack. All interfirm transactions are carried through the banks, and by watching the credit and debit entries (which correspond to enterprise sales and purchases, respectively), banks can determine whether the transactions occur on schedule.

In the area of institutional studies of the Soviet system there now exists a vast and competent literature.[4] Excellent works also exist on the development of the Soviet system from its beginnings to the latest administrative reforms.[5] The statistical, institutional, and historical studies give the Western reader a comprehensive picture of the Soviet economy. Though many points of fact are not yet settled, we cannot claim to be in the dark about what goes on behind the Iron Curtain.

Studies of alien forms of economic organization frequently concentrate on the malfunctioning of systems. In such an approach it is all too easy to exaggerate the diseases and to condemn the entire organism because it is not completely healthy. Excessive concern with pathology is characteristic of professional critics on both sides of the Iron

[4] See, for instance, Joseph S. Berliner, *Factory and Management in the USSR*, Cambridge, Mass., Harvard University Press, 1957; Franklyn D. Holzman, *Soviet Taxation: The Fiscal and Monetary Problems of a Planned Economy*, Cambridge, Mass., Harvard University Press, 1955; Robert W. Campbell, *Soviet Cost Accounting*, unpublished Ph.D. thesis, Harvard University, 1955.

[5] A standard work is M. H. Dobb, *Soviet Economic Development since 1917*, London, Routledge & Kegan Paul, Ltd., 1948.

Curtain. These critics fail to see the organism for the disease and expect any moment that the organism (on the other side of the curtain) will collapse and die. Nevertheless, used in moderation, the comparative pathology approach shows where the unresolved problems and chief pressures lie.

While the present study touches upon institutions, refers to some pathological manifestations of the soviet-type system, and even ventures to compare the system's efficiency with that of the free-enterprise economies, the approach is primarily analytical.[6] The purpose of the analysis is to show how the soviet-type economy allocates resources, that is, how it decides upon the product mix, the method of production, and the distribution of the product. This method of study, when applied to a soviet-type economy, requires explanations and disclaimers.

The analytic approach developed by economists in capitalist nations concentrates on the study of the market mechanism. Allocation through governmental action, which takes place jointly with market allocation in all capitalist countries, plays a peripheral role in the analysis. At most, economists investigate how government decisions influence and modify the market process. The decisions made by the government are taken as a datum; the investigation of the decision-making process is left to political scientists.

The conventional division between economics and political science cannot be preserved in a study of the soviet-

[6] Among a number of analytical studies now extant, mention should be made of Robert W. Campbell, *Soviet Economic Power*, Boston, Houghton Mifflin Company, 1960; and Gregory Grossman (ed.), *Value and Plan*, Berkeley, Calif., University of California Press, 1960.

type system. Techniques developed by economists to study the market have little relevance to a system in which the market (as we know it) plays a vestigial role. Economics as a study of allocation of scarce resources to conflicting needs of society is powerless when the needs are expressed through a central plan. We may inquire about the political pressures brought to bear upon the policy makers or about the policy makers' psychological or ideological makeup. We certainly are not able to use economic techniques built upon the assumption that there is a multitude of decision makers, each pursuing his own aim.

In dealing with the problems of planned economies, the economist must abandon most of the tools of contemporary analysis. This does not mean that he has to give up analysis altogether. Even a completely centralized system faces decisions which fall into the realm of economic analysis. Plans are not made in a vacuum; they are drawn in response to the needs of the moment. There must be a method (no matter how crude or arbitrary) for determining priorities. Orders must be transmitted; their execution must be controlled; mistakes must be corrected. The mechanism might be clumsy compared with the elegance of the market mechanism (or should one say, compared with the elegance of the mechanism as portrayed by economic textbooks), but it is there, nevertheless. The economist has no special insight into the policy makers' psyche, but he has a comparative advantage in the investigation of the mechanics of the system.

A word of defense has to be said about the use of the awkward term "soviet-type system," a term chosen by elimination, since all the alternatives, such as "communist system," "socialist system," or "planned economy system" are likely to be more misleading. The soviet-type system was evolved in the U.S.S.R. and adopted by Russia's European allies. The economies of other communist countries, such as China and Yugoslavia, are markedly different, not to mention the economies of socialist countries such as Norway or Sweden or the planned non-soviet economies like India.

Because the key role in a soviet-type economy is played by the Party leaders, it is proper to inquire at the outset into the Party's goals. This is the purpose of the next chapter. The same chapter relates how the structure of the soviet-type economy is adapted to serve the Party's goals.

Chapter 3 deals with the role of individuals as sellers of labor and purchasers of goods and services. The consumers and the workers in Soviet-bloc countries enjoy a broad area of freedom of choice. The analysis of the aggregate effects of consumer and worker choices comes closest to conventional free-enterprise economics. Yet, even here this analysis cannot be pushed too far, since the individual choices have no direct influence on production decisions. What to produce and how to produce is decided by the country's leadership, and the decisions are reflected in the national plan.

The technique of planning and the method of planning are described in the next two chapters. Chapter 4 is devoted to perspective and long-range plans which map out the broad outline of development and change. The current functions of the economy are directed by annual plans, described in Chapter 5.

The first five chapters set the stage for a discussion of the operation of the economy. They outline the theory underlying the system, the role assigned to consumers and to workers, and the method of preparing national plans. How the plans are put into operation, how they are enforced, and how performance is controlled—in short how the economy functions—is the topic of Chapter 6. An appraisal of the efficiency of the system is given in the closing chapter. The same chapter compares the achievements and the shortcomings of the soviet-type system with the achievements and shortcomings of free enterprise economies.

The soviet-type system has now been in existence for over forty years. From modest and halting beginnings it has developed into a complex and viable structure. The system can boast of startling achievements, but it is plagued by many failures. The achievements and the failures and the history of the system and its present state are worthy of thorough investigation. This short essay, giving a brief analysis of the functioning of the system is, like all primers, an invitation to further study.

2

Economic Decision Making

In a soviet-type system, the structure of the economic institutions and the allocation of economic resources are determined by the political leadership. The leadership's decisions are influenced by the needs and wishes of the population and by internal as well as external economic and political pressures, but the paramount role is played by the policy makers' goals.

The purpose of this chapter is to inquire into the aims of the policy makers in the Soviet-bloc countries and to show the interrelation of these aims with the economic system. Methods of planning, administration, and centralization or decentralization of economic decision making will be considered in the light of the Communist Party's goals.

a. Policy Goals in a Soviet-type Economy

The underlying tenet of the soviet-type systems is that the Communist Party is the sole repository of truth and the sole representative of national interest. The correct functioning of the system requires "unqualified confidence in the economic directives laid down by this [workers'] government." [1] The government's directives must be followed explicitly if national interest is to be served.

To understand the economic policies pursued by Soviet-bloc countries, one must gain some insight into the goals of the governing Party. Two basic types of documents serve as a primary source: economic plans and pronouncements of Party leaders.

"The economic life of the USSR," says article 11 of the Soviet constitution, "is determined by the state national economic plan." The same holds true for the other soviet-type economies. Economic plans are a concrete expression of the leadership's wishes and serve as orders for action. Thus a study of plans reveals the preferences of the policy makers, much as a study of markets in free-enterprise countries reveals the preference of the consumers.

Unfortunately, a study of economic plans does not result in a complete and unbiased view of the aims and preferences of the leadership. Economic plans are operative documents which reflect the policy makers' goals as well as the constraints within which the plans are built. Unless one

[1] Stanislav Strumilin, *Planning in the Soviet Union*, London, Soviet News Booklet 17, p. 11, 1957.

knows the nature of the constraints, one can all too easily mistake a measure dealing with a specific problem for an over-all goal.

The division into "goals" and "constraints" is useful, though somewhat artificial. The distinction is clear when both goals and constraints are economic entities expressible in physical terms. A goal of rapid steel expansion must be compatible with the physical constraints on the availability of coal, iron ore, and other factors of production. The issue is not so clear when either the goals or the constraints, or both, are structural and not economic. For instance, as recently reasserted in Poland, "small scale private production is needed and even essential" in the early stages of Communist rule, while later on "it becomes a drag on social and economic development." [2] At an early stage small-scale production should be promoted, but later it must be suppressed. The policy makers' dislike of private production is surely as strong in the period of promotion as in the period of suppression. The constraints have changed. At first nationalized industry is incapable of replacing small-scale private production; hence the latter must be encouraged. With the improvement of state industrial organization, the functions of private industry can be taken over. Should private enterprise continue to be more efficient than state enterprise, its presence would tend to subvert the system.

Official and unofficial pronouncements of Party leaders,

[2] Mieczysław Rakowski, *Zagadnienia planowania wieloletniego w Polsce Ludowej*, Warszawa, Polskie Wydawnictwa Gospodarcze, 1955, p. 25.

as well as Party policy statements and resolutions, give a broader view of Party aims and are less affected by the needs of the moment. For instance, the nationalization of all means of production and the collectivization of agriculture are stated Party aims, even in the periods in which private enterprise is tolerated. Yet policy pronouncements tend to be vague and are permeated with emotive statements with no immediate relevance to reality. The well-known goal of the ultimate "withering away of the State" is an example of a statement with little or no operational meaning. Thus, to discover which statements have a counter-part in concrete policy, one is forced to look at concrete plans.

The process of discovering the leadership's goals requires a comparison of concrete plans and statements of Party purpose. In the plans, the goals are obscured by the constraints and requirements of the moment. In the policy statements, goals are hidden beneath verbiage. By using both types of documents, one can, at best, reach some conjectural conclusions concerning the policy makers' intentions, yet the process is essential in reaching an understanding of the soviet-type economy.

The general goal of economic planning, says article 11 of the Soviet constitution, is "to raise the material and cultural standards of the working people," and to ensure the independence and security of the nation. To give empirical content to such a statement, it is necessary to inquire into the economic assumptions concerning the improvement of living standards. Professor Brus suggests:

A fundamental assumption, often explicitly formulated by political leaders and by theorists is that the fastest possible growth rate is the best possible method of satisfying economic as well as political needs.[3]

According to Brus, the Soviet leadership equates improving living standards with rapid accumulation. The statement finds ample corroboration in Soviet literature.[4] A review of the economic plans also reveals that soviet-type economies devote a larger proportion of resources to investment than do free-enterprise economies.

While rapid accumulation may ultimately result in higher living standards, rapid investment leaves fewer resources which can be used to satisfy current consumption needs. In times of weakening of communist rule (as in Russia following Stalin's death and in Poland and Hungary during the period from 1955 to 1957), the rate of investment decreases and more resources are devoted to consumer goods. We may suspect that policy makers have a higher investment preference and a lower consumer goods preference than the consumers taken collectively.

Full employment figures prominently among the goals of Soviet leadership. As stated in the *Manual of Political Economy* of the Soviet Academy of Sciences, "the planned Socialist economy excludes unemployment and guarantees the full employment of the entire labor forces of the economy." [5]

[3] Włodzimierz Brus, *Ogólne problemy funkcjonowania gospodarki socjalistycznej*, Warszawa, Państwowy Instytut Wydawniczy, 1961, p. 117.

[4] Thus Strumilin states that the economic policy goal "is the distribution of existing production resources and manpower so as to ensure the *highest* degree of crisis-free expansion at the *highest* possible rate," *op. cit.*, p. 9.

[5] The Economic Institute of the Academy of Sciences of the

In this the socialist economy differs radically from the capitalist system which (according to Marxist analysis) "inevitably produces unemployment which, for the capitalists, is a method of creating a cheap labor force." [6] Officially there is no unemployment in any of the Soviet-bloc countries.

The principle of full employment is not followed unconditionally. The possibility of frictional unemployment accompanying technological progress is now recognized in the Soviet Union. When introduction of new production methods leads to reduction in the labor force, temporary idleness is a cost which has to be borne.

In Poland, where low productivity and high labor turnover are often blamed on the excessive ease of finding jobs, there are people who feel that some unemployment might be beneficial to the economy. The principle of full employment is universally accepted, but it is not absolute. At times it must yield to the principle of efficiency.

Economic equality is another important policy goal: "From each according to his ability, to each according to his need," is probably the best-known communist slogan. Nationalization of the means of production eliminates property income and serves the equality goal. Whether current wage policy also promotes equality is not so clear. In Poland, effective wage differentials are extremely small, probably much smaller than in any capitalist country. In the Soviet Union, after a brief experiment, the equaliza-

USSR, *Manual of Political Economy*, 2d ed., 1955, quoted from the French edition published as Académie des Sciences de l'URSS, Institut d'économie, *Manuel d'économie politique*, Paris, Éditions sociales, 1956, p. 466.

[6] *Ibid.*, p. 466.

tion policy was abandoned in favor of substantial wage differentials. The differentials are justified in terms of incentives needed during the "lower" stage of communism, i.e., during socialism. In that period, not all workers are fully aware of the social nature of work, and they need personal incentives.

In times of extreme necessity, to raise production the communist principle of equality gives way completely to the need for incentive payments. Thus while the 8th Congress of the Communist Party of Russia underlined the necessity of providing subsistence means to the entire population,[7] the 9th Congress stated that:

> The system of wage payments must become one of the powerful incentives to competition. The system of payments must be linked with the distribution of food: as long as the Soviet Republic lacks food resources, the hard-working and diligent worker must be better provided for than the sluggard.[8]

The "work-or-starve" policy no longer is practiced either in the Soviet Union or in the other "socialist camp" nations; however, the principle of reward differentiation persists. In Poland, where the trend toward equality is further advanced than in the other countries of the "camp," attempts are made to increase wage differentials in order to give greater work incentives.

The mere recording of plans and policy moves would

[7] See Institut Marksa-Engelsa-Lenina-Stalina pri Z.K. KPSS, *Kommunisticheskaia partiia Sovietskogo Soiuza v resoliutsiakh s'ezdov, konferentsii i plenumov Z.K.*, Moskva, Gosudarstvennoye izdatel'stvo politicheskoi literatury, vol. I, p. 410, 1954.

[8] *Ibid.*, p. 481.

lead us to the conclusion that equality is a subordinate goal, giving way to considerations of productivity. Indeed, it is possible that equality, like the "withering away of the State," is a political slogan empty of empirical content. It is possible, on the other hand, to entertain the notion that equality is contingent upon the achievement of a certain income level. To achieve that level, accumulation is necessary; to foster accumulation, it is important to give work incentives. Thus the equality goal may be of prime importance, but its achievement must be delayed. Here we are again in the realm of conjectures.

Collective ownership of all means of production is a proximate goal of all communist parties, and it is not to be delayed until a hypothetical "higher" stage of communism is reached. Nationalization of all means of production is a prerequisite for unitary soviet-type planning. Unless all means of production are government-owned, it is impossible to run the whole economy like "one big factory":

> In order to draw up an effective plan for the whole of a nation's national economy it is necessary in the first place to organize it as a unified economy. In the USSR, where all the means of production belong to one owner, to the Soviet people, and where the national economy is really an integral unit, like a big factory with numerous departments and shops, but with a single office, all the necessary conditions exist for the compilation, and what is even more important, for the implementation of a single national economic plan.[9]

Nationalization of all means of production, states Marxist doctrine, is a prerequisite for the construction of a "class-

[9] Stanislav Strumilin, *op. cit.*, p. 4.

less society." [10] To establish unity of interests and to abolish
class distinctions, it is necessary to eliminate the conflict
between tool owners and tool users through national ownership. National ownership fulfills yet another role: It concentrates economic power within the hands of the Party.

Despite its crucial importance, the policy of nationalization does not follow a consistent trend in Soviet-bloc countries. Private ownership of means of production was reintroduced in the Soviet Union under the New Economic
Policy and, on a much more modest scale, in Poland after
the 1956 "revolution." In both cases some degree of control
over resources was sacrificed for the sake of economic
efficiency.

Agriculture provides an extreme example of compromise
in the matter of public ownership. Collective farms are
regarded as inferior to direct state ownership, and collective farmers form a separate "class," distinctly inferior
to the workers. The collectives are preserved because of
production needs. In Poland, even private land property
is tolerated. The collectivization drive from 1949 to 1955
decreased agricultural output and put a brake on further
industrial investment. To permit continued industrialization it was deemed expedient to decollectivize. In the
future, when industrialization is pushed far enough to permit large-scale mechanization of agriculture, collectivization
or even direct state ownership of land might be possible (so
the leaders hope) without adverse output effects.

Some of the goals of the policy makers are purely economic and can be expressed in production targets. Others

[10] Russian Communist Party (b), 8th Congress. See Institut
Marksa-Engelsa-Lenina-Stalina, *loc. cit.*

are institutional and are concerned with the organization of the productive system and of society. Marxist doctrine states that institutions are inseparable from economic results, and that doctrine exerts an influence over soviet-type economic planning. A plan, as Kuybishev stated at the 17th Conference of the Communist Party of Russia, should say what should be done and how it should be done. The action and its framework are inseparable:

... the essence of the plan lies precisely in that it should indicate not only the ultimate aim but also the ways of its achievement, the instruments of implementation of this plan, and how the implementation should take place in time and space.[11]

Since institutions are doctrinally inseparable from economic results, many policies are pursued with both kinds of goals in view. The policy of rapid industrialization, for example, has institutional aims in addition to the purely economic ones.

Industrialization is rapidly promoted in the belief (shared by many non-communist economists) that it provides the only road to rapid economic growth. Industrialization is also necessary to consolidate Communist power. According to a pronouncement at the 12th Congress of the Communist Party of Russia, "industrialization alone lays the unshakable foundations of dictatorship of the Proletariat." [12] The industrial workers, not the farmers, are the backbone of the regime. To consolidate the regime, the number of workers must grow in relation to the other occupations.

[11] Quoted by Stanislav Strumilin, *op. cit.*, p. 12.

[12] Russian Communist Party (b), 12th Congress. Institut Marksa-Engelsa-Lenina-Stalina, *op. cit.*, p. 687.

Industrialization also provides another example of the flexibility of communist policy. Excessive industrial investment at the cost of agricultural investment weakens the economy. To restore the nation's ability to feed itself, one may need to curtail some ambitious industrial plans in order to invest in agriculture. Such shifts have taken place in several of the communist countries since Stalin's death.

Doctrinal assertions notwithstanding, institutional and economic goals may be competitive rather than complementary. The institutional goal of concentrating power in the hands of the Party may run against the economic goal of efficient production. Agriculture provides the clearest examples. There can be little doubt that the institutional goal (collectivization) conflicts with the goal of efficient agricultural output. In the Soviet Union of the 1930s, agricultural production was sacrificed to achieve collectivization. In postwar Poland, the opposite course was adopted. Though collectivization was and is a goal of the Polish Communist Party, it was decided to introduce it slowly so as not to disrupt production. Indeed, when collectivization in the late 1940s and early 1950s diminished agricultural output, a number of collectives were dissolved to improve agricultural efficiency.[13]

[13] It is questionable whether Soviet Russia's leadership was aware at the onset that collectivization would cut down output. The collectivization drive was undertaken for political and social reasons and also to force the farm sector to deliver more food to the cities. The fact remains that the policy was pushed ruthlessly even after the adverse effects became amply apparent. Collectives also became the model of agricultural organization for all the Soviet-bloc countries.

In Poland, decollectivization was triggered off by political

The flexibility of policy in the face of changing constraints is an acknowledged and important ingredient of
Communist rule:

Our plans are determined in a given stage not only by the
economic but also by the political tasks of the moment. The fulfillment of these tasks frequently requires from us the sacrifice
of various economic interests of secondary importance for the
sake of achieving more important political tasks of the moment.[14]

It is tempting to conclude on the basis of comparisons of
different plans that the policy makers' preferences are subject to frequent changes. It would be false, of course, to
assume that preferences are immutable. On the other hand,
the external constraints often change faster than the preferences. For instance, shifts of emphasis from heavy industry to consumers' goods and back again (such as have been
observed over the last fifteen years in several communist
countries) are more likely to result from internal and external political pressures than from basic policy changes of
the Party.

A search for constants in a pragmatically shifting policy

---

events, yet the leadership of the Polish Communist Party is fully
aware that output increased thereby. Collectivization remains
an aim of the Polish Party leadership, but its introduction must
await a propitious social situation, as well as technological improvements. With the present attitude of the peasantry and the
current methods of cultivation (virtual lack of machinery which
would permit mass cultivation), collectivization would cut down
output—a risk which the Party is unwilling to take.

[14] Stanislav Strumilin, "Zakon stoimosti i planirovanie," *Voprosy Ekonomiki*, July, 1959, p. 128.

turns all too quickly into a game in which all the solutions appear to be equally true. Every policy change may be interpreted as a change in the policy makers' preferences. Alternately, every change may be interpreted as a reflection of external constraints imposed upon an immutable leadership. Party pronouncements may be either dismissed as propaganda or looked upon as the real expression of the will. Conversely, plans either are revelations of the true intentions of the leadership or are measures suited to the need of the day which reveal little or nothing about long-range goals.

Among so many uncertainties and so many policy shifts, one goal stands out clear and changeless: the preservation of Communist power. To preserve power the Party may be forced to retreat from complete nationalization and collectivization or to settle for a low rate of economic growth. It may have to tolerate economic inequality or unemployment. All goals may have to be sacrificed, except the goal of preservation of power.

The maintenance of Communist Party rule as the supreme goal of soviet-type systems has the sinister connotations of a plot to fool and abuse the public. This is not the case. Communist theoreticians are the first to acknowledge that Communist rule takes precedence over all other considerations. Because economic goals are contingent upon Communist rule, the preservation and strengthening of the rule is the first consideration of the system.[15]

[15] There is a vast literature concerning the political aims and assumptions of communism. An excellent synthesis, which includes the most important statements of Lenin, Stalin, minor party theorists, and theoretical statements of leaders of the satel-

b. Planning and Administration

Methods of economic planning and administration evolved in the Soviet Union and in other countries of the Soviet camp are designed to fulfill economic functions designated by the leadership. The technical side of resource allocation through planning will be considered at length in a later chapter. In this section I shall look at planning and administration as tools in the policy makers' hands, and I shall consider them in the light of the policy objectives, the most important of which is the preservation of Communist power.

The translation of economic programs into concrete plans is the task of technicians whom I shall call planners. Planning cells exist at all levels of the soviet-type organization, down to the level of plants and factories. The most important planning functions are accomplished at the central level by a national planning commission.

Planners working in the national commission are middlemen between the policy makers and the operative level of the economy. Their role is to devise programs which are feasible and acceptable to the policy makers. The planners express policies in concrete terms. They also investigate the constraints (such as the productive capacity limitations) within which the production targets must be fitted and inform the policy makers about the state of the economy.

The ideas and suggested solutions of the planners may be

---

lite nations will be found in Adam Łopatka, *Kierownicza rola Partii Komunistycznej w stosunku do państwa socjalistycznego,* Poznań, Wydawnictwo Poznańskie, 1960.

accepted, modified, or rejected by the policy makers. The planning officials, in their role as technicians, have no choice except to follow the Party leader's wishes in the preparation of the final version of the plan.

Once the plan is approved, it becomes the blueprint for action for all levels of the economy. The operative units, from the ministries in charge of industry groupings down to enterprises making individual products, receive their orders through the medium of the plan. The planners are not responsible for the broad outline of policy, but they must answer for the technical competence of their product.

Economic plans are valid for stated periods of time, and new plans are issued at regular intervals. The institutional goals of the leadership, on the other hand, are not put into a single document, and there is no one organization which is in charge of institutional planning. What can be called the "institutional plan" (parallel to the "economic plan") must be culled from laws, directives, administrative ordinances, and customary procedures. Such documents have an indefinite life and are valid until superseded by new directives.

The institutional as well as the economic plans of all the Soviet-bloc countries evolve over time with the accumulation of experience. A vast gulf separates the current Soviet Seven-Year Plan from the modest beginnings of Goelro in the 1920s. By and large all the Soviet-bloc countries emulate the Soviet Union's pattern, since the U.S.S.R. is politically dominant and has the longest history of planning. Only China and Yugoslavia—the two countries which are not politically dominated by Moscow—depart markedly in their planning from the Soviet system. Differences between, say, Poland and East Germany are minimal. The basic goals of the ruling parties in the two countries are the same. The planning methodology is almost identical. Actual plans differ somewhat, since there are different socioeconomic and political constraints in the two countries. For instance, the imposition of a Soviet institutional pattern (including complete nationalization of agricultural property) is more difficult in agrarian Poland than in the more industrialized East Germany.

The post-Stalin policy of "different roads to socialism" recognizes that plans must be adapted to local circumstances. The goals are the same in all the countries as are the planning techniques. The detailed content of plans differs (whereas under Stalin even plan content was almost the same, regardless of local circumstances), but details are of little concern in this study, which aims at an over-all analysis of the functioning of a soviet-type economy.

Having distinguished between policy making and planning, it is useful to make a further distinction and to consider economic administration as a separate entity. Planning is a technical department to top policy makers. Administration is their executive branch. The administration is responsible to the policy makers for the execution of the plans drawn up by the planners. There is thus a clear division of responsibility: The planners are responsible for the cogency and correctness of the plans, and the economic administrators are responsible for plan execution.

In practice there are many functional and personal connections between planning, administration, and policy making. The administrators have a voice in the creation of plans, since it is they who will have to carry out the program. The policy makers, on the other hand, interfere with the administration and change it when necessary. Many of the top administrators and planners sit on high policy-making councils and participate in the decision-making process. Yet, despite all these connections, the distinction among the three functions should be clearly kept in mind.

The pattern of administration in soviet-type economies undergoes frequent changes [16] and differs from country to country. An uninitiated observer who notes such changes is apt to draw the conclusion that there is also a great diversity in the pattern of policy making and in the techniques of planning. Such a conclusion is in most cases quite unwarranted.

Administrative diversity, in the face of underlying similarity of economic systems may be illustrated by the example of the Soviet Union, Poland, and Czechoslovakia. Since the Khrushchev reforms, the Soviet Union, Czechoslovakia and also East Germany have been administered along regional lines. Poland and some of the other satellite nations retain a centralized system rather reminiscent of Stalinist centralization in the Soviet Union. On the other hand, Poland, like Yugoslavia, has Workers' Councils which on paper have considerable administrative power. Thus, if

[16] In the Soviet Union during the postwar period "change has been the rule rather than the exception" at the top planning level as well as at the ministerial level, says Herbert Levine. Yet planning methodology has been scarcely affected by the changes in the formal administrative system. See Herbert Levine, "The Centralized Planning of Supply in the Soviet Union," in Joint Economic Committee, *Comparisons of United States and Soviet Economies*, United States Government Printing Office, 1960, pp. 153ff.

one took the differences in the administration at face value, one might conclude that Polish administration is a hybrid of centralism and workers' rule, while the Soviet Union and Czechoslovakia are ruled along regional lines. In fact, however, the differences in decision making are quite superficial.

Some of the administrative differences are simply a matter of convenience. Regionalization of the immense Soviet territory carries more advantages and fewer disadvantages than regionalization of Poland. Yet such an explanation is not complete. Khrushchev's decentralization of Soviet administration had a deep symbolic meaning: It indicated dramatically a break with Stalin's system. The decentralization, unlike the decentralization of the Soviet economy in the initial postrevolutionary period, was reconciled with a continued centralization of policy making and with over-all central planning.

In Poland the 1956 "revolution" was also accompanied by administrative changes. Some of these were purely symbolic, as the change in the name of the Central Planning Commission. Others were thrust upon the administration by spontaneous forces. Of these the formation of the Workers' Councils is a prime example. The Councils were formed in the midst of the revolutionary fervor and for a while played some role in the administration of enterprises. The Councils' powers were gradually curtailed as the Communist Party regained control of the situation. In name they still remain as part of the administrative system, but their role is now minimal. Still other reforms were instituted to improve efficiency and diminish the degree of centralization. Enter-

prises received the right (which in 1959 and 1960 was curtailed and now is of no significance) to make certain investments out of their own funds without central authority.
The authority over some enterprises was transferred to
regional and local bodies. Enterprises were grouped into
consortia which, on paper, have substantial autonomy.
Some of these reforms are purely a matter of convenience.
Others reflect changes in decision making and planning.
Still others are symbolic and empty of any operational content.

It is highly dangerous to deduce from the formal pattern
of administration—or from changes in that pattern—where
and how economic decisions are actually made and what
the chains of command are. The Polish system looks on
paper like a parliamentary democracy with a mixed economic system. In fact, there is a single-party rule, and with
the notable exception of agriculture, the economy is almost
completely nationalized.

Under the official rules of behavior, all Polish economic
plans must be presented by the executive for approval by
a multiparty parliament. The plans are discussed by parliamentary committees and become law only after approval by
majority vote of the chamber. In interim periods, between
plans, the executive may issue economic decrees, but as a
broad rule, all major proposals have to be submitted to
Parliament for action.

Within the executive branch the formal lines of authority
run from the Cabinet of Ministers through the ministers in
charge of branches of the economy (such as agriculture,
light industry, heavy industry, etc.) to the vice-ministers in

charge of smaller subdivisions of the system. Each ministry is staffed with permanent employees in addition to the appointed heads.

Below the governmental level, there are groupings of enterprises which form separate administrative units. The current Polish system consists of a two-tier organization. Enterprises which carry out the same or similar activities are grouped into consortia which have some planning and administrative functions. The enterprises themselves are legal corporate entities, fully owned by the state. Some types of economic activity, for instance hotels and restaurants, are controlled by regional and local administrative bodies and are only loosely supervised by the central administration.

While the Polish constitution assigns to the Communist Party the role of *primus inter pares* in the task of governing the country and building socialism, the Party in reality rules supreme. As in the Soviet Union, and unlike any parliamentary country, the Party's powers transcend the powers of parliament and the government executive. Whether the Party chooses to rule through a centralized or a decentralized administration is of no substantive importance. The administration is there to carry out the Party's orders; if need be, the administrative chain may be short-circuited or the administrative system changed.

Parliamentary approval of economic measures is routine. It is true that certain measures are occasionally changed or improved after discussion by parliamentary committees. Much more frequently, however, Parliament is called to approve measures which have been in force for some time without the official knowledge of the legislative branch.

The executive branch of the government functions in the economic sphere as an administrative branch of the Party. The economic plans, prepared by the Planning Commission, incorporate the Party's directives and must gain the approval of the Party before being put into effect. When the government ministers issue economic decrees, they clear their action with the Party, not with the Parliament. On occasion the Party even issues orders to lower administrative levels without going through the Cabinet.

The changes which took place in Poland in the period from 1955 to 1957 did not alter in any radical way the real structure of decision making. Perhaps the greatest change consists of increased emphasis on "socialist legality," i.e., on work through properly constituted channels. Direct Party interference, such as the overriding of administrative orders by Party functionaries, is now the exception rather than the rule. The increased decentralization of power is, however, largely illusory. Where real decentralization took place—as in the case of the Workers' Councils—the changes were wiped out as soon as the danger of an upheaval was past.

Sceptical comments concerning the real meaning of administrative decentralization should not be pushed too far. A centralized administrative system is best adapted to a centralized system of decision making. Conversely, administrative decentralization carries with it a measure of decentralization of power. It is important to note, however, that while the soviet-type system is compatible with a variety of administrative patterns, it puts very rigid limits on the permissible degree of decentralization of decisions.

To maintain its sovereignty the Party must have the

power to allocate the economic resources of the nation. This fundamental fact puts rigid bounds on the structure of the soviet-type system. The nature of these bounds and how much power can be surrendered by the Party without destroying the system are the topics of the balance of this chapter.

c. Party Sovereignty and the Decision-making Process

In a soviet-type economy the Party maintains the prerogative to make all key economic decisions; however, this prerogative should not be confused with complete freedom of action. The decision makers, even under a stringent dictatorship, are subject to pressures and influences which reflect upon the decision.

The Party leaders do not make their decisions in a vacuum; they take into account popular wishes and weigh them in some fashion before deciding on a policy course. Precisely how the population's desires are weighed cannot be determined empirically. The formation of a policy makers' "utility function" and the inclusion in that function of the "utilities" of other groupings is an entertaining but rather idle game.[17]

[17] It is sometimes claimed that the policy makers attempt to maximize their preference function. This would be so if the policy was made in isolation. In fact, the policy is a compromise between the leaders' preferences and the preferences of other members of the group. Unless one specifies the interaction between the leaders and the other members it is idle to talk about "preference functions."

It might be useful to think of decision making in a soviet-type economy in terms of a Western family unit. In both cases resources are apportioned to present and to future needs. A further division concerns the satisfaction of collective needs and individual needs. The decisions may be made dictatorially by the family head or after consultation with the other family members. In either case it would be improper to say that the decision maker ignores the needs and desires of the family members.

In a Western family, as in the soviet-type economy, the sovereignty of the decision maker rests on his control over major sources of income. Where other family members have their own sources of income, the control is correspondingly lessened.

Comparing diverse families (which have the same basic decision-making pattern), one may observe differences which arise in respect to consultation, to the application of set rules in reaching a decision, and to the delegation of decision-making powers.

The decision maker may arrive at his decisions in a purely arbitrary fashion, or he may follow certain set rules of behavior and allocate resources in accordance with some scale of urgency of wants. He may consult the other members of the household, or he may make the decisions without any formal consultation. Finally, the decision maker may concern himself with all the details of the consumption pattern, or he may divide resources into broad categories and let other members handle the details.

The simile between decision making in a soviet-type economy and in a family unit should not be carried too far lest it prove misleading. It is useful, however, to see the interrelation between control over resources and sovereignty and to note the variations (and the permissible limits) of consultation, decentralization, and application of set rules in the Soviet decision-making pattern.

The concentration of power in the hands of Party leadership varies with the strength of the Party's position. Historical circumstances (such as real or imagined danger of foreign invasion, the character of the Party leadership, etc.) also affect the pattern. Typically (but not inevitably) non-Communist decision makers must be tolerated during the initial period following the establishment of Communist rule. In the second phase, when power is consolidated, the non-Communist elements are liquidated. This stage requires ruthless action and strong centralization. Complete consolidation and the formation of Communist technical cadres permit a relaxation of rule.

In transitional stages to communism (especially in the so-called "people's democracy" stage) a multiplicity of divergent interests must be accommodated if the economy is to function. There are smallholders, artisans, and members of liberal professions. Ultimately all of them will disappear, and the Party will express the unitary purpose of society. While the transition lasts, the minor interests receive a voice (they can even elect deputies to Parliament), provided the supremacy of the Party is ensured.

During the transition, the plan which maps out the economic activities of the nation is not all-embracing. While there are vestiges of capitalism, there must also be vestiges of market production. Ultimately all production will be nationalized, and production for profit will cease, as was foreseen by the 12th Congress of the Communist Party of Russia.

In Poland, the Communist take-over in 1945 and 1946 was followed by a period of mild control, in which small industry, agriculture, and retail and wholesale trade were permitted to follow their own course, that is, to produce for profit. This period of laxness was justified in terms of incomplete Communist control. The fiction of "coalition" government was being preserved because a wide basis of popular support (or at least nonopposition) was needed to help establish Communist rule.

During the period of cold war from 1949 to 1955, Communists attempted to eliminate all vestiges of capitalism from the Russian satellite nations. To accomplish their task, they had to resort to extreme centralization. The managerial personnel, largely inherited from pre-Communist regimes, was "bourgeois tainted." Communists put in managerial posts were incompetent. The few available managers who were loyal and reasonably skillful had to be concentrated on the top of the administrative ladder, while lower-level management was reduced to clerical functions in which competence and loyalty matter very little.

The extreme centralism and concentration of power in the hands of a small group of top Party leaders led to great inefficiency. Even before Stalin's death it became apparent that administrative changes were necessary, and that minor policies must originate (as well as be implemented) on lower levels. Stalin's death precipitated the changes. To avoid open revolt, the leadership's grip on the economy had to be relaxed.

Relaxation of the rule consisted primarily in letting sub-ordinate administrators make their own decisions on matters which are of no immediate concern to the economy. Before the reforms each producing unit was shackled by a myriad of obligatory "indicators," and no variations in their products (either in inputs or in outputs) was permitted without central authorization. Each manufacturing unit had to obey no less than eighteen separate directives concerning such matters as the fulfillment of the physical plan, the value plan, the labor plan, the raw materials plan, etc. After 1956 the list was radically curtailed and the discretionary powers of management were increased; although by Western standards, company managers still have very little room in which to maneuver.

The decentralization of decision making which took place in 1956 was possible because by that time the Party could rely on moderately well-trained and reasonably loyal administrative cadres. With a loyal staff it became possible to give up some rigid controls without abandoning any real power and to regain the confidence of the people without capitulating to the people.

Formal consultation of Party leadership with lower cadres and other groupings within the economy fluctuates with the degree of central control. When all decision making is concentrated at the top consultation plays a minor role. During the period of "collective leadership" which followed Stalin's one-man rule, consultation received increased emphasis. Now, prior to the announcement of any major change in economic policy, special meetings are held to acquaint Party personnel and workers with the proposed changes. Economic programs are also discussed at great length at Party congresses, where delegates frequently voice proposals and demands.

The limits of the rank-and-file power to propose, and of the power of the Party leadership to dispose, are clearly indicated by the Party leaders themselves. Summing up the discussion at the 3d Congress of the PZPR, Gomułka took note of the numerous suggestions and stated that:

> The appropriate Party and Government authorities are committed to consider the proposals in detail. They will decide on their practical usefulness, that is, on the possibility of putting them into practice.[18]

Consultations with both the Party cadres and the people increase the Party's ability to put its program into practice. Plans and policies are no longer thrust upon an uninformed (and possibly reluctant) public. They are explained, their rationale is understood, and they receive a measure of support.

The policy makers are, inevitably, influenced by those whose opinions they consult. This does not mean that they abandon their sovereignty. The consultative opinion can always be overruled since the power to decide remains in the leadership's hands.

There remains the problem of the relationship between Party sovereignty and reliance on set rules of economic decision making.

An extremist concept of Party sovereignty equates sovereignty with the ability to take completely arbitrary action.

[18] W. Gomułka's speech at the 3d Congress of the Polish United Workers' Party (hereafter referred to as PZPR), see *III Zjazd PZPR*, Warszawa, Książka i Wiedza, 1959, p. 997.

The concept originated during the period of war communism and enjoyed undisputed primacy during the last years of the Stalinist era. All rules of conduct are rejected, for the policy maker must have complete freedom of choice. The "all powerful Socialist state" can act with "complete arbitrariness." Under such a concept "the science of political economy of socialism could be reduced to a number of practical rules of procedure," [19] that is, to a codification of the customary modes of action of the leadership of the Party.

The extremist concept of policy makers' freedom of choice excludes the possibility of any rational economic calculation:

When social production is administratively determined there is the possibility of only two kinds of decisions. These two possible types of decision arise in any administrative system: at the top level there are political decisions mapping out the goals, and at the bottom level technical decisions determining the method of carrying out the tasks. In such a system there is no room for economic decisions and for economic calculus.[20]

The system of complete arbitrariness found its apologists among economic theoreticians. Thus Professor Minc gives the following rule for the determination of the efficiency of investment in a socialist state:

[19] Z. Fedorowicz, "O problematyce teorii pieniądza w gospodarce socjalistycznej," *Finanse,* vol. 11, no. 2, p. 17, 1960.

[20] Stefan J. Kurowski, *Szkice optymistyczne,* Warszawa, Pax, 1957, p. 288.

The choice of investments is decided by the political and economic tasks put before society on a given level of development by the Government and the Party of the working class.[21]

This means, in effect, that investment efficiency is measured by the priority assigned to the investment by the policy makers. Attempts to discover rational rules of procedure in a planned economy pose a grave threat to the absolutist planning concept:

An over-all indicator of the effectiveness of investment was feared the most. Such an indicator was particularly dangerous because it could become an instrument of economic choice and would *automatically* . . . disqualify some investment projects and select others. Such a criterion would threaten the very foundations of the power of the practitioners who made their decisions on uncontrolled and uncontrollable grounds.[22]

and again:

All theoretical attempts to define . . . investment criteria were rejected, because the acceptance of any one criterion would have limited the freedom of investment-decision choice. The argument was also used that no single criterion can take into account all the factors on which decisions must be based.[23]

The desire to keep the power of arbitrary decision making breeds a need to back decisions with valid and universal

[21] Bronisław Minc, "O efektywności inwestycji w gospodarce socjalistycznej," *Ekonomista,* January, 1951.

[22] Kurowski, *op. cit.*, p. 293.

[23] *Ibid.*, pp. 292–293.

"laws." As Kurowski put it: "Practitioners who managed very well in their activity without relying on economic theory felt the need for scientific and theoretical *ex post* justification of their actions." [24] The "justificatory laws" were especially abundant in the years of absolutist planning. They still are exceedingly numerous and enjoy a preferential status compared with scientific hypotheses.[25]

The justificatory laws designed to give "scientific" backing to political decisions can either be restatements of observed behavior of the leadership or statements of certain problems facing the economy. An example of the latter is the "basic law of socialism," which is "the insurance, through uninterrupted growth and improvement of socialist production on the basis of the highest technique, of the ever-growing material and cultural needs of society." [26] This "law" is a statement of purpose which can justify any mode of action whatever.

Actual rules of behavior often receive justification in terms of the "basic law" or of the pronouncements of im-

[24] *Ibid.*, p. 296.

[25] Since the 1956 "October Revolution," the Polish Party leadership has been quite reluctant to quote "laws" which might sound false to the public. For instance, at the 3d Congress of the PZPR, Gomułka emphasized the need for the use of the most modern production methods available, but cautioned that "the principle of the prime importance of modernization should not be raised to the rank of an absolute law." See *III Zjazd PZPR*, p. 105.

[26] J. Stalin, *Economic Problems of Socialism in the USSR*, New York, International Publishers, 1952, p. 32. Quotation from the Polish edition, Warszawa, Książka i Wiedza, 1952, p. 44.

portant leaders. In the *Manual of Political Economy* of the Academy of Sciences of the USSR, we read about a "law of development of priorities" which is tantamount to the "law of faster development of branches producing producers' goods relative to branches producing goods for individual consumption." [27] This "law" is justified in the Manual by a pronouncement of Khrushchev, though it antecedes Khrushchev's rule by many years. In the course of his struggle for power, Khrushchev denounced the opposition (which favored a faster rate of growth of consumer's goods) for their misunderstanding of Marxism-Leninism and in the course of his denunciation stated the law. The law, clearly, was stated *in order to justify policy decisions,* and the decisions in no way depend on the so-called law.

The law of the faster development of branches producing producers' goods relative to branches producing goods for consumption is particularly useful whenever the leadership decides to accelerate investment. Ever since the Soviet First Five-Year Plan, investment has received high priority in all soviet-type economies, and heavy use has been made of the law.

If needed, the law of development priorities can be modified or even abandoned, as in Poland in the period from 1954 to 1957. In 1954 it became apparent that the ambitious investment program mapped out under the Six-Year Plan would have to be cut down. There was widespread dissatisfaction with the declining living standards. The investment program itself was too hastily planned and too poorly co-

[27] The Economic Institute of the Academy of Sciences of the USSR, *Manual of Political Economy,* 2d ed., 1955 (French edition), p. 443.

ordinated to be feasible. The first move, then, was to diminish the tempo of investments. In 1954 it was decided to place less emphasis on investment, while preserving the basic idea that investments should grow faster than consumption. To justify the move, the law of priorities was revamped as follows:

The law of socialist industrialization, and of enlarged production in general, is the faster rate of growth of means of production (group A) than of consumers' goods (group B). The more backward the country, and the lower the producers-goods base, the more the rate of growth of the means of production must surpass the rate of growth of consumers goods.[28]

In other words, the progress made during the first years of the Six-Year Plan permitted a slowdown of the rate of capital accumulation without violating the "law."

By October, 1956, it became eminently clear that the modest deemphasis of investment was not enough. During 1957 and 1958, consumers' goods production was permitted to expand at a faster rate than investment goods production, and the law was not quoted. The industrialization rate was speeded up again in 1959, but this time it was deemed wiser not to cite any "laws." Instead, the leadership merely asserted the "paramount importance" of the capital goods' industry for the whole economy.[29]

Whenever the "law of development priorities" fails to

[28] Speech of B. Bierut at the 2d Congress of the PZPR. See *II Zjazd PZPR*, Warszawa, Książka i Wiedza, 1954, p. 52.

[29] See Stefan Jędrychowski, "Wytyczne rozwoju gospodarki narodowej w latach 1959–65," *III Zjazd PZPR*, p. 341.

apply, the "law of balanced economic growth" can be invoked. This law states the problem of harmonious development of all branches of the economy. It neither defines "harmony" in precise terms nor does it say how "harmony" is to be achieved. Its vagueness is a ready justification for any kind of investment decision.

The absolutist concept of Party sovereignty is now rejected, though it still has its supporters in the Soviet Union and in the other countries of the socialist camp. By now it is freely admitted that planning must take place within limits imposed by resource availability. In the Soviet Union limiting factors are included under the general category of "nonantagonistic contradictions" which arise in socialist systems. The Soviet economist Y. A. Kronrod discusses the nonantagonistic contradiction between investment and consumption which arises in the process of "broadening socialist reproduction." Excessive consumption slows down growth by limiting investment. Excessive investment can slow down growth, too, if consumption is limited to such an extent that reproduction of the labor force is endangered.[30]

The relaxation of the assumption that planning is all-powerful has led to a revival of economic studies. Under Stalin it was impossible to study the effects of investment on consumer welfare. The issue was settled once and for all by the statement that "socialism eliminated the antago-

[30] Y. A. Kronrod, "O protivorechiack v razvitii sotsialisticheskoi ekonomiki i putyakh ikh razreshenia," in K. V. Ostrovityanov et al. (eds.), *Voprosy stroitel'stva kommunizma v SSSR*, Moskva, Akademia Nauk, SSSR, 1959, p. 286.

nism between consumption and investment, which is an at-
tribute of the Capitalist system." [31] At most one could study
details of the investment program without questioning its
general lines. Many other questions, for instance the inter-
dependence of agricultural and industrial growth, were
similarly closed to economic investigation. Economics was
reduced to a laudatory "science."

Policy makers now understand that the output of food
puts a limit on the rate of industrial growth in a closed
economy. Recognition of this fact has led to studies of the
supply elasticity of agriculture in Poland and to studies of
the relations between investment in agriculture and food
output. Such studies in turn might provide the policy
makers with information useful in reaching allocative decisions.

The trend toward increased acceptance of the reality of
economic constraints leads to the problem of a fully "rational" planned system in which arbitrary action would be
completely eliminated. Several theoretical models of rational allocation in a socialist economy have been devised
by West-European and American economists in the 1930s.[32]
A brief glance at the best-known scheme, devised by Oscar

[31] The Economic Institute of the Academy of Sciences of the
USSR, *Manual of Political Economy,* 2d ed., 1955 (French edition) p. 456.

[32] See H. D. Dickinson, "Price Formation in a Socialist Com-
munity," *Economic Journal,* vol. 43, June, 1933; Abba P. Lerner,
The Economics of Control, New York, The Macmillan Company,
1944; and Fred P. Taylor and Oscar Lange, *On the Economic
Theory of Socialism,* Minneapolis, University of Minnesota
Press, 1938.

Lange, will show why such rational socialism remains unacceptable to Soviet leadership.

The purpose of Lange's scheme is to eliminate the social inequities of capitalism and to introduce a depression-free system while preserving the freedom of consumer choice. Social equality is fostered through the nationalization of all means of production. Nationalization, and a planned investment policy, eliminates crises and permits continuous economic growth. At the same time, consumer wishes are followed and the product mix responds to aggregate demand of consumers.

Under capitalism consumer control over the product mix is highly imperfect. Producers enjoying a measure of monopoly power are able to restrict output in order to achieve private gains at the expense of the consumers. Lange proposes to increase the degree of consumer sovereignty by instituting a quasi-market functioning in accordance with rules of perfect competition.

The Lange scheme envisages that managers of nationalized enterprises would be required to maximize their profits at given factor and product prices. In the absence of any control over prices, each manager would behave as though he were working under perfect competition. Workers in the Lange scheme would sell their labor in accordance with their preferences, while consumers would buy the goods of their choice. Thus workers' choice and consumers' choice are preserved. Indeed, since the system responds to worker and consumer wishes, workers and consumers are "sovereign."

The major innovation proposed by Lange is that the role

of the market should be taken over by a Planning Board. In day-to-day operations the Board would be required to announce prices, which would serve as a framework for decision making by the workers, the consumers, and the managers. In a free competitive market the price tends to equalize supply with demand; Lange's price setters would be required to act as if they followed the market rules.

Lange foresees cases where the Board's price policy would have to depart from free-market rules in order to foster social goals. For instance, competitive-market rules fail to apply to industries with long-range decreasing marginal costs, such as pipelines and electric transmission. According to Lange such industries ought to be run at a loss in order to preserve the rule of marginal-cost pricing which leads to the most efficient resource use. Appropriate pricing could also be used to encourage consumption deemed especially beneficial to society and to discourage consumption of harmful goods.

In deciding on the global volume of investment, the Planning Board does not have to follow market considerations. On the contrary, the system has the alleged advantage of freeing aggregate investment from the vicissitudes of the market. In allocating investment funds among the various branches of the economy, however, the Board would take into account the signals given by the market. In industries where there are no significant indivisibilities, high profits are a sign of underinvestment, while low profits are a sign of overinvestment. The investment policy could be guided by these signs.

The Lange scheme of democratic socialism is an antithesis of the soviet-type system. In a soviet-type economy, the Party is sovereign; in the Lange system the powers of economic leadership are strictly circumscribed. In the soviet-type system, the plan outlines the production schedule; in the Lange system, consumer wishes are followed, except when social desiderata dictate a different course. Soviet-type nationalization changes the economy into "one big factory." Managers of individual enterprises follow the orders transmitted from the top. Nationalization in the Lange scheme preserves the independence of the productive units. Each unit behaves as it wishes, and rewards and punishments are meted in accordance with an abstract and mechanistic scheme.

What makes the Lange scheme totally unacceptable to communists is that Lange's system is mechanistic and leaves virtually no room for arbitrary action. Lange's Planning Board could readily be replaced by a computer solving the equilibrium price problem by successive approximations. Even the departures from market prices could be programmed. There is no room for the all-powerful leadership which represents social interest. Each individual continues to pursue his own aims, as under free enterprise. Indeed, except for the elimination of property income and for control over investment, the Lange system is a free economy.

The need to preserve decision-making power puts definite limits on rationality in the economic process and on the degree of decentralization in a soviet-type economy. Even such a radical advocate of economic calculus as Professor Brus puts very rigid limits on the scope of the calculus:

All economic decisions in a socialist country can be divided into three categories. The first are the basic macroeconomic decisions which must have the character of direct central authority decisions. The second are decisions concerning individual consumption, given the income level, and decisions about the choice of employment, and place of work. These decisions (except in unusual periods) must be decentralized and carried out through the market mechanism. The third group are decisions often termed "current economic decisions" (and concern such matters as the size and structure of production in individual enterprises and industrial branches, the source of inputs, the character of minor investments, the details of the manner of employee compensation).... if models, i.e., forms of organization of the socialist economy, are really to correspond to the basic tenets of the system, they may differ from each other only with respect to the extent of centralization or decentralization of the third decision group.[33]

This quotation defines the maximum limitations on arbitrary policy makers' powers which can be imposed within a soviet-type system. The basic decisions *must* remain in the policy makers' hands, and there can be no question regarding their rationality or irrationality. The debatable question is whether minor assortment decisions can be made through the automatic rules of economic calculus or whether they, too, are to be decided on policy grounds.

The quasi-market mechanism advocated by Western proponents of democratic socialism in the 1930s and 1940s is clearly incompatible with Soviet ideology and the aims of Soviet leadership. The organization of the Soviet system must leave the fundamental decision-making powers in the leadership's hands. If the leadership is to be the only rep-

[33] W. Brus, *op. cit.*, pp. 113–114.

resentative of public interest, it must have the freedom to decide and it must be able to translate its decisions into action. The soviet-type plan cannot become a mechanistic device, but it must express the Party's will.

Any market, even a quasi-market of the Lange type, puts great limitations on the freedom of choice of the political leadership. The market indicates what is to be produced, and the indicators are not under the policy makers' control. It is true that the market can be manipulated by the policy makers, but even so, production for the market destroys the direct relation between the Party leadership and the activity of the productive units in the economy. One can even go further: If the market signals are disregarded, the existence of a market constitutes a threat to the Party leadership. Discrepancies between market signals and policy makers' decisions show that the interests in a society are not congruent with Party wishes. Because this possibility cannot be entertained in a system in which the Party represents the sovereign will, the market mechanism cannot be tolerated.

The refusal to abandon voluntarism for automatic resource allocation does not necessarily signify the rejection of all methods of rational resource allocation. Under Stalin's rule, techniques of mathematical economics were virtually banned; however, the current regimes promote research in these methods. At present, as in the West, mathematical programming is applied to relatively narrow problems of product mix and factor proportions within an individual enterprise. It is possible that improvements in computation techniques and in computers will permit the programming of over-all plans. Such programming would be acceptable to the leaders, provided that they can dictate the final goals and make the decisions. Rational methods of calculation are acceptable if they preserve the leaders' prerogatives, but they must be rejected if they lead to the reinstatement of the consumer as the supreme arbiter.

d. Summary and Conclusions

The purpose of all economic activity in a socialist state is the service of society. The interpretation of social interest is the prerogative of the Communist Party. The Party leadership decides how to serve society, and what economic activities to engage in. The leadership's decisions are embodied in economic plans and in institutional plans. The economic plans are drawn up by planning technicians; the plans become the rule of economic action for the administration and for the operating levels of the system.

The Party leadership in a soviet-type system is the seat of economic power, and the planners as well as the administrators have a dependent position. The leadership's decisions are, of course, dependent to some extent upon the wishes of the Party members, the administrators, the technicians, and the public at large. The decision-making system may be likened to the Western family unit in which the head of the unit allocates resources and is influenced by the needs of the various members of the group, as well as by the pressures which are exerted on the decision maker. Nevertheless, the head of the group has the ultimate right to decide, and this right is guaranteed by his control over resources.

The goals of the Communist Party may be pursued within

a variety of systems, ranging from Stalinist autocracy to the relative decentralization of control of the current "collective leadership" phase. Communist rule is incompatible, however, with any system which provides a standard of allocation independent of the leadership's desires. The market, be it a capitalist market or a quasi-market devised by democratic socialists, is, as such, an independent device. The market can be tolerated as a transitional phenomenon in the period of Communist take-over, but it cannot be built into a planning system.

The economy of a Soviet-bloc state receives its orders from the Party leadership and cannot receive any counter-orders, be it from a market or a computer. New techniques of economic calculus will in time be adopted by the system. As long as the Party rule is preserved, such techniques will become tools in the Party's hands. They will be used to translate more effectively the leadership's will into action and to foster the supreme goal, the preservation of Communist power.

3

The Position of Workers and Consumers

The place of the individual in a soviet-type economy is defined by the postulate that the Communist Party is the only repository of social interest. According to Marxist theory the socialist revolution eliminates the conflicts of interest which exist under capitalism. With all means of production belonging collectively to the nation, there can be no conflict between employers and employees or between consumers and producers. Production is for use, not for profit. There is no problem of division of the product between tool owners and tool users because all the tools belong collectively to the workers. The unitary interests of society are embodied by the plan designed and approved by the Party.

According to the Marxist doctrine, the conflict-free soci-

ety can exist only under socialism. The socialist state "takes
into account the various needs of society. The state develops and improves productive techniques . . . in accordance
with society's growing needs. . . ." [1] The individual in his
capacity as worker pursues aims common to the entire
society, and the state, under the leadership of the Party,
satisfies the needs of individuals as consumers. In free-
enterprise economies—still according to Marxist doctrine—
there is an inherent conflict: free enterprise is based on the
relation of "inequality between the exploiter and the ex-
ploited." [2] In such a society, there can be no harmony, only
a continuous struggle. The worker is the object of exploitation by the capitalist. The consumer is not the goal of productive activity, but merely a source of profits.

Shorn of its propaganda elements, the Marxist view reveals a profound difference between the Soviet and the
free-enterprise concept of the role of the consumer and the
worker. Soviet doctrine asserts the monistic character of
society. The free-enterprise concept shows a pluralistic
society in which consumers, workers, and producers pursue
their particular aims. The Soviet state decides upon the
product mix and the distribution of the product; under free
enterprise, the product mix and distribution result from the
actions of the various interests in the economic and political
sphere.

[1] The Economic Institute of the Academy of Sciences of the
USSR, *Manual of Political Economy*, 2d ed., 1955, quoted from
the French edition published as Académie des Sciences de
l'URSS, Institut d'économie, *Manuel d'économie politique,*
Paris, Éditions sociales, 1956, p. 448.

[2] *Ibid.*, p. 132.

Conceptually, the clearest image of the role of consumers and of workers in a free-enterprise society emerges from the consideration of an idealized perfectly competitive system. Such a system, according to Adam Smith and the eighteenth-century Scottish school, corresponds to the "natural order" and results in "social harmony." Modern economists are reluctant to say that any system, no matter how perfect, is natural or harmonious. Still, it can be readily proved that under perfect competition it is impossible to improve the welfare of any individual, without decreasing the welfare of some other individual, and that by pursuing his individual aims each individual fosters the well-being of society. In that restricted sense a competitive system is efficient and harmonious.

Western concepts of "consumer sovereignty" and what by analogy could be defined as "worker sovereignty" are intimately connected with the functioning of the idealized competitive system. Such concepts have no place in the monistic society envisaged by Communist leaders. It is therefore useful to say a few words about the nature of such "sovereignty" before turning to the Soviet scheme.

By consumer (worker) sovereignty we mean the automatic adjustment of the production pattern to the aggregate choices made by the consumers (the workers). Each consumer makes the decision of how much and how to spend. The consumption decisions are guided by the prevailing prices, and the sum of all the individual purchases amounts to the total purchase basket. Producers adjust their production in accordance with the market signals. They concentrate on profitable products and cut back the output of unprofitable items. By attempting to maximize their profits, producers adjust their supply to the urgency of the market demand. Similarly, the workers seek jobs with the highest real wage. Wage differentials reflect, on one hand, the relative urgency of need of the producers and on the other the preference of workers for diverse kinds of jobs.

It would be out of place to repeat here *in extenso* the theory of competitive resource allocation and income division. Suffice it to note that competitive markets provide an automatic mechanism (1) for the adjustment of production to the collective wishes of consumers and workers, and (2) for the remuneration of productive factors in accordance with their marginal productivity, i.e., in accordance with their social contribution.

The competitive mechanism gives no guarantee that each individual, or even the majority of individuals, will be pleased with their income position. Moreover, individuals may be dissatisfied with the price structure which the competitive market yields. This dissatisfaction often leads to the abandonment of competitive action in favor of collective action either through monopolistic association or through noneconomic channels.

It may be claimed, indeed, that consumer sovereignty is of no importance to the individual in modern society. The individual is concerned with his own income and with his personal freedom of choice. It matters little to him what mechanism determines the income level and how prices are fixed. As long as the individual must take the wage level as a parameter and as long as prices of consumption goods are fixed, it makes no difference whether the levels are determined by competition or through administrative action.

This line of reasoning leads to the mistaken conclusion that there is no difference between the position of the consumer and of the worker in free-enterprise and Soviet-bloc countries. It is true that a consumer in a soviet-type economy is free to choose his purchase basket (housing being the one major exception). It is also true that workers are permitted to choose their jobs. Thus there is consumer (and worker) choice in the soviet-type system as well as in the free-enterprise system. The similarity ends there.

The major difference between the two systems, as far as the seller of labor is concerned, is that under free enterprise the worker's reward is determined by his work, while in a soviet-type economy there is no necessary connection between the two. Although "payment according to the quality and quantity of work" is accepted as a principle of wage determination, it is a principle for the guidance of the wage setters, not a part of the automatic allocation mechanism. The principle can be (and is) modified by the policy makers. In essence, the worker contributes to the state and is paid by the state an amount determined by the state.

A more fundamental difference affects the collectivity of consumers and workers. The Soviet approach severs all connection between the aggregate preferences of consumers and the product mix. Production is determined by the national plan, and the plan does not automatically respond to consumer wishes. It may be, for instance, that everybody could be made better off by switching production from shoes to shirts, but no such switch is planned. A well-functioning competitive market does not guarantee that income will be distributed to everybody's liking, but it does guarantee that (barring technological progress or capital accumulation) the well-being of any individual cannot be increased without decreasing the well-being of another individual. A soviet-type system does not guarantee even that.

It is absurd, and also quite unnecessary, to claim that, in practice, the market in a free-enterprise economy conforms to the competitive ideal. The fact remains that the free-enterprise system possesses a built-in allocative mechanism. That mechanism may function more or less efficiently, and it can be modified through deliberate policy action. The soviet-type system is devoid of such a mechanism. Allocation by the state in accordance with the needs of the citizens provides no guidance for the measurement of these needs. Yet decisions have to be made in some way by the policy makers and the planning authorities. These decisions are influenced, of course, by the wishes of workers and consumers. The purpose of the present chapter is to explore how wage and consumer goods production decisions are reached in a regime in which there is consumer and worker choice and in which decisions rest with a group of policy makers.

a. Work and Wages

The Soviet approach toward the problem of wage determination stems from the Marxist doctrine according to which all value is created by labor. Under this doctrine it is meaningless to calculate the marginal productivity of the various factors. All product is created by labor and all product is ascribed to it. The division of product is determined by the community's needs, not by factor contributions.

The division of income is determined by the policy makers on behalf of the unitary interests of the community. The economic plan determines how the workers will dispose of the goods and services made available through their efforts.

Workers in the socialized sector of a soviet-type economy contribute their work to the state and receive payments from the state. The wage payments are determined by the economic plan and represent the portion of the product which is made available for the satisfaction of individual needs. The policy makers decide on the size of the wage bill and on the division of the wage payments. The share of the product not paid out in wages is devoted to the satisfaction of collective needs and accumulation.

The divorce of the individual contribution of the worker to the national product from the payments made to the individual worker gives the policy makers much flexibility in the allocation of labor resources. In a free-enterprise country a worker is not employed (barring public works projects) unless the addition to the value of the product attributable to the worker exceeds the wage. In a soviet-type economy there is no necessary connection between the worker's contribution and his pay.

The planned wage scheme permits the soviet-type economies to maintain full employment. As in the Western nations, full employment is deemed desirable from a social point of view. In addition, it has long been held that "the planned development of a national economy necessitates the maximum exploitation of the nation's labor force." [3]

[3] See Russian Communist Party (b), 8th Congress, Institut Marksa-Engelsa-Lenina-Stalina, pp. 410ff.

The employment of any person—it was believed—contributes to national well-being, no matter how small the individual contribution.

It is evident that the limits of useful employment in a soviet-type economy are broader than in a free-enterprise system.[4] Under capitalism an employer will not hire a worker for $1 per hour if the worker's product is worth only 50 cents. Hiring at 50 cents per hour may be prohibited by legal minimum wages. Even in the absence of minimum wages, no one will hire a worker whose product is less than the wage needed to keep the worker alive. A Soviet state, on the other hand, will benefit from hiring any worker whom the state keeps alive, as long as the worker's output is greater than zero.

Work in soviet-type economies is a right as well as an obligation. Except for the incapacitated, no person receives an income without working. Conversely, any person capable of work may obtain a job. Indeed, until quite recently it was officially held that in the Soviet Union (and by extension in the other Soviet-bloc countries as well) "unemployment has been liquidated fully and forever." [5]

Full employment in soviet-type economies is achieved through a combination of labor-allotment and wage fund-

[4] This point receives much emphasis from socialist writers on both sides of the Iron Curtain. See, for instance, M. Dobb, *Economic Growth and Planning*, New York, Monthly Review Press, 1960, *passim*, and Mieczysław Kabaj, "Mechanizm zatrudnienia w gospodarce socjalistycznej," *Ekonomista*, no. 1, 1960, pp. 52ff.

[5] N. G. Alexandrov, quoted by Emily Clark Brown in "A Note on Employment and Unemployment in the USSR in the Light of Technical Progress," *Soviet Studies*, vol. 12, no. 3, January, 1961.

allotment policies. Every enterprise has an employment plan and is permitted to hire up to the number of workers specified in the plan. The plan also specifies the basic wage per worker employed. Thus, up to the planned level of employment, the wage fund is proportional to the number of workers employed, and labor is a free good to the individual enterprise.

The individual enterprise has every incentive to hire a full contingent of workers. The larger the work force, the easier it is to meet the production targets. Since all the workers as well as the management receive bonuses for fulfilling and for overfulfilling the production quotas, it is in the interest of the enterprise to hire as many workers as permitted.

The relation between the labor plan and the production plan is established on the basis of planning norms. These norms, in turn, are based on a study of actual work performance and on the appraisal of effects of technological changes. Performance influences the norms; hence it is tempting for the enterprises to build up a "reserve army" of workers and to "hoard" labor.[6] Moreover,

... the demand for an excessively large labor contingent ... is used by management to hide its incompetence. ... Excessively large demand for labor is treated as insurance against the attrition of workers.[7]

To make sure that it will have a sufficient number of workers to accomplish its prescribed tasks, an enterprise overstates the labor requirements. Surplus labor is free,

[6] Mieczysław Kabaj, *op. cit.*, pp. 61–62.
[7] W. Daszkiewicz, "Problemy planowania werbunku siły roboczej," *Gospodarka Planowa*, vol. 7, no. 11, 1952.

while a labor deficiency is costly to the management as well as to the workers; hence overstatement of needs is the rule.

The first effects of the introduction of employment policies characteristic of the soviet-type systems are a rapid elimination of unemployment and a drainage of available labor supplies. In Poland, nonagricultural employment increased by 2.5 million between 1947 and 1952,[8] i.e., the number of non-agricultural workers doubled in five years. There is little doubt that such a "mobilization of the labor force" has many positive effects, though a substantial proportion of the labor is likely to be misallocated.

The immobility of population may leave pockets of unemployment even if the "general mobilization" policy is successful. People may be unwilling to leave their place of birth, or movements may be impeded by housing shortages in the developing region. The over-all full-employment policy must be supplemented by a policy of industrial location or a policy of population transfer. Both policies are adopted to some extent. To facilitate the employment of the idle workers, a special intervention fund was formed in Poland in 1956.[9] This fund is used to make investments in areas of excess labor. In addition, steps are taken to provide housing for migrants to labor deficit areas.

It is the success of the soviet-type employment policy which creates new problems and necessitates the search for new solutions. Countries such as Poland, which suffered perennially from unemployment and from surplus agricul-

[8] Bolesław Bierut, *O umocnieniu spójni między miastem a wsią*, Warszawa, Książka i Wiedza, 1952, p. 37.

[9] See J. Obodowski, *Zatrudnienie*, Warszawa, Polskie Wydawnictwa Gospodarcze, 1959, pp. 56ff.

tural population, are transformed within a few years into economies with a labor shortage. It then becomes necessary to switch from a policy of employment at all cost to a policy of labor economization.

To achieve over-all economies in the use of labor, it is necessary to tighten the norms governing the output-worker ratio, and/or to provide enterprises with incentives to reduce the number of workers. Either scheme is unpopular with the workers for either scheme increases the work load. Since the over-all wages fund is fixed according to plans, there is no automatic linkage between labor economies and labor remuneration; hence work load increases are even less palatable. Nevertheless, a norm-tightening and labor-saving incentive policy is pursued with increasing vigor in the countries of the Soviet camp.

The actual schemes for labor economizing differ from country to country and even from industry to industry. The Polish construction industry may serve as an example.[10] Between 1951 and 1958, the wage fund in the industry changed in proportion to the physical production goals. Such a linkage led to a rapid expansion of employment in the face of mounting labor shortages. Moreover, since not all types of production are equally labor intensive, it was possible to greatly overstate the demand of labor. An individual enterprise's plan would foresee a relatively high proportion of labor-intensive production, and the enterprise would be authorized to hire a large contingent of workers. In practice, an assortment switch would occur; the propor-

[10] Lesław Mastan, "Bankowa kontrola funduszu płac w przedsiębiorstwach budowlano-montażowych," *Inwestycje i Budownictwo,* vol. 11, no. 1, January, 1961.

tion of work requiring less labor would mount, thus permitting plan overfulfillment and leading to bonuses. To remedy the situation, rigid assortment control was in force between 1958 and 1960. Finally, in 1960, a rule was instituted prohibiting each enterprise from surpassing a stated wage fund. With the institution of a rigid wage fund, there is incentive to economize on labor, provided wages per worker can be increased. Such increases—within narrow limits—were authorized.

Labor shortages have induced the leadership in the Soviet-bloc countries to abandon their rigid defense of full employment. In fact, a small percentage of unemployment is now officially fostered. In the Soviet Union, it is recognized that technological change may create unemployment. Workers cannot be kept on jobs made redundant by mechanization, lest the advantages of mechanization be lost. The workers who are technologically displaced may have to seek new jobs or even migrate to other cities.[11]

The full-employment policy was also relaxed in Poland to improve the on-the-job performance of the workers. Vacant jobs and insignificant differences in wage and working conditions have encouraged Polish workers to drift from job to job and to do the least possible amount of work on each job. When a worker who quits or who is dismissed suffers a modicum of idleness and income loss, his performance is likely to improve.[12]

[11] See Emily Clark Brown, *op. cit.*

[12] Absenteeism provides one of the measures of laxity in work. In 1955 absenteeism averaged 274 hours per industrial worker. In 1956 and 1957 absenteeism increased to 289 and 316 hours respectively. See Halina Diamand, *O polityce za-*

The measures to economize on labor and exact better work from those who are employed represent a step back from the "general mobilization" policy, which solved unemployment problems that periodically plague free-enterprise countries. In the long run the policy is wasteful, and it must give place to a policy of economizing, lest the production goals be defeated. The problem of economization of resources (which will be discussed at length in Chapters 6 and 7) is still far from being solved in the soviet-type systems. Yet one thing is already clear: Full employment of all human resources is not costless. Some human resources may have to be idle, if the idleness is necessary to improve the efficiency of other workers.

In the soviet-type economies, a clear distinction must be drawn between the regulation of demand for labor on the part of enterprises and the wage policy. Although each enterprise is a separate accounting unit, the wage fund is administratively determined, and changes in the wage fund are of no immediate concern to the enterprise. The wage level and the method of wage payments affects, of course, the workers. Thus wage policy operates on the side of supply of labor but not on that of the demand for labor.

Except in times of emergency, workers in the Soviet-bloc countries are free to choose their own jobs. Wages must therefore accomplish an allocative function. Workers must be distributed among industries and enterprises in accordance with demand. Within each industry and enterprise, workers must be allocated to various tasks according to their qualifications.

---

trudnienia w świetle uchwał XI Plenum KC PZPR, Warszawa, Książka i Wiedza, 1958, p. 11.

Wages, as already noted, also provide incentives for the individual. Historically, much more attention has been paid to the incentive-giving than to the allocative role of wages. The emphasis on allocation came with the gradual tightening of the labor market during the 1950s.

Since wage payments are (at least in theory) the only means of livelihood for the able-bodied, wages must provide a socially acceptable living standard. This consideration places a floor under the wage level.

Finally, wages are used as a method of reward for the socially approved individuals and professions. An individual (or a profession) which, in the eyes of the policy makers, deserves special praise receives higher wages than one which is frowned upon.

The diverse goals of labor policy inevitably lead to difficulties and compromises. It is safe to say that there is no general wage policy, but instead there are diverse policies which vie for supremacy and replace each other depending on the needs and pressures of the moment. The balance of this section will be devoted to a discussion of some of the major issues at hand and the attempted solutions.

Two conflicting general principles of wage determination accepted by Marxist ideology complicate and confuse the design of a rational wage policy. One is the Marxist principle which advocates payment according to need. The other is the "Leninist principle of payment . . . according to the quantity and quality of work." [13] The two principles stand in clear contradiction to each other, and neither of

[13] See Zofia Morecka, "Płaca w gospodarce socjalistycznej," in O. Lange (ed.), *Zagadnienia ekonomii politycznej socjalizmu,* 2d ed., Warszawa, Książka i Wiedza, 1959, pp. 497–498.

them agrees with rational labor-resource allocation through the wage mechanism.

The "Leninist principle" is commonly (though incorrectly) identified with piecework. Piecework rates reward each individual according to the quantity of work which that individual performs on a given job. It is exceedingly difficult to set these rates so that the pay for different jobs is equalized. Indeed, this and other difficulties have resulted in a gradual retreat from the piece-rate system. While up to the 1950s piece rates played a paramount role, the current tendency is to treat them as an incentive payment given in addition to a basic flat rate. In occupations in which the unit of work cannot be readily defined, flat rates are now preferred.

The retreat from piecework schemes occurred for reasons well understandable to Western labor economists. A piecework system must be connected with a system of performance "norms." The norms are set to give extra payment to the exceptional worker only. As performance improves over time (be it through improved techniques, better methods of administration, improved skills, or even for reasons external to the enterprise, such as raw materials), the workers' wages rise automatically. To cut back payments, it is necessary to readjust the norms every so often. Such readjustments cause dissatisfaction. If carried out too often, the readjustments defeat the purpose of the piecework system. Workers who know that their norms will be increased if they work too hard are likely to ration their effort.

Whenever the basic rates are set at a very low level, there is a tendency on the part of management to help workers by setting up fictitious norms. Occurrences of this

sort are rife throughout the Soviet zone and are known
euphemistically as "laxity of work discipline." [14]

A comprehensive piecework system is bound to interfere with the allocation of labor according to supply and demand considerations. Posts with low base pay and high
piecework earning possibilities may be more attractive than
posts where the pay rate is high, but the piecework earnings
are low. When such a situation develops, an adverse selection is likely to take place. Highly skilled and able workers
prefer "lower" situations which give the possibility of extra
earnings, while less competent workers will choose "higher"
posts with better base pay. [15]

Table 1 *Basic wage scales and workers' earnings in a
Polish textile mill*

Base pay of each grade of workers (złotys per hour)	Average monthly earnings	
	Least efficient workers (złotys)	*Most efficient workers (złotys)*
3.00	700–800	1700–1800
3.20	700–800	1500–1600
3.80	800–900	900–1000
4.00	800–900	800–900
4.30	1500–1600	2300–2400
5.50	1100–1200	1400–1500

Source: Wiesław Krencik, "O politykę płac zapewniającą maksy-
malne wyniki produkcji," *Gospodarka Planowa,* 1958, no. 12.

The distorting effect to piece rates can be illustrated by
the example of a Polish textile mill. The workers in the mill
are grouped into six grades. The base pay of the highest

[14] See Gomułka's speech at the 2d Congress of the PZPR, *II
Zjazd PZPR,* p. 100.

[15] See H. Diamand, *op. cit.,* pp. 20ff.

grade surpasses the base pay of the lowest grade by 83 per cent, yet the actual earnings of the most productive workers in the lowest grade are some 17 per cent higher than the earnings of the most productive workers in the highest grade. The differential in grades is reflected only in the pay of the least efficient workers of each group, as illustrated in Table 1.

Attempts to rationalize the wage system are very numerous. Periodic reforms diminish the importance of piece rates and restore base rates to their proper place. A recent wave of reforms throughout the Soviet-bloc countries attempted to restore the balance, as shown in Table 2.

These reforms prove ephemeral. Even if a reform restores

Table 2   *Basic wages as percentage of total earnings of workers in the Soviet Union, Rumania and Czechoslovakia*

	Before the 1957–1958 reforms	*After the 1957–1958 reforms*
U.S.S.R.		
Coal mining, Donets Basin	66	71
Iron and steel industry	56	77
Nonferrous metals		
(piece-rate workers only)	55–60	70–75
Chemical industry	48	70
Rumania		
Average for nationally		
planned industry	62	79
Czechoslovakia		
Range for the entire industry	50–53	75–90 *

* Projected in the wage reform of 1958.
Sources: U.S.S.R. and Rumania, *Socialisticheskii Trud,* 1958, no. 5–8. Czechoslovakia, *Życie Gospodarcze,* 1958, no. 41.

the desired relation between base wages and piecework payments, the relation is likely to be distorted with the passage of time. Gradually work norms become outdated and piecework payments increase. In jobs in which productivity increases are slow, work discipline must be relaxed if wages are to keep up with the wages of the more fortunate individuals.

A successful solution of the base rate piecework dilemma does not automatically yield a rational wage structure. Two individuals might be performing work identical in quantity and quality, yet their services might not be needed with equal urgency. Indeed, the principle of equal pay for equal work applies only when the supply and demand conditions are identical. If wages are to allocate labor, they must reflect differences in supply and demand. This issue is not clearly perceived by the policy makers of the Soviet world:

... there exist substantial discrepancies in the wage levels of diverse branches of the Polish economy. Clearly, it is difficult to estimate the correct proportions of wage levels. We have very little experience in this sphere and there is a lack of definite criteria for judgment.[16]

The search for criteria all too often takes the form of comparison with the wage scales prevailing abroad. Such

[16] Michał Krukowski, *Aktualne problemy płac w przedsiebiorstwach socjalistycznych,* Warszawa, Książka i Wiedza, 1958, p. 16. Krukowski's pamphlet is a reprint of a lecture given at a lecture course organized by the Department of Propaganda and Agitation of the Central Committee of the Polish United Workers' Party. Thus the opinion represents authoritative Party circles, rather than the opinion of competent economists. It is significant

comparisons are made in order to provide "a proper, objective view of the situation." [17] The comparisons have some validity only if the supply and demand conditions are similar. Very often they are not.

The social valuation of diverse occupations is clearly reflected in the relative wage levels of manufacturing industries and other occupations. Marxist doctrine divides labor into productive, i.e., labor giving rise to material goods, and nonproductive, i.e., labor in service industries. The former is deemed more valuable than the latter. Furthermore, more emphasis is put on the production of means of production than on the production of means of consumption. The wages set by the Polish national plan for 1958 reflect the differences in social valuation. Of all industrial workers, textile workers are the lowest paid and coal miners the highest. Letting average textile workers' wages equal 100, the average wage in coal mining equals 217. Wages in the other consumers' goods industries rank above the textile workers' wages, but below the wages of the capital goods' producing industries. School teachers' wages average 119 and are lower than the wages of workers in any heavy industry. Medical doctors in the public health service are paid 154, i.e., somewhat more than the average pay in the machine tool industry (144) but less than the workers in the steel tool industry (164). These differences, it is freely admitted, are the result of a policy which "put special emphasis on industry ... and neglected the pay of teachers and health officers."

---

that even in the writings of professional economists, the allocative role of wages is never clearly stated.

[17] *Ibid.,* p. 18.

The policy was a consequence of the postulate that "pay should reflect the importance of the given kind of work to the national economy," [18] the importance being understood here in terms of the Marxist priority of productive over non-productive labor and of producers' goods over consumers' goods.

A glance at the Polish wage scales reveals that the range of pay is exceedingly small, especially for a country suffering from an acute shortage of specialized personnel. Although averages are often misleading, it is striking that in 1957 the average pay of engineers with university degrees in the machine-tool industry was only 48 per cent higher than the average pay of the workers in the same industry. The differential was largest in the light (consumers' goods) industries; yet, there too, engineers' wages were only double the average wages of the workers.[19] In many industries the wages of skilled workers surpassed the wages of the supervisory personnel.

In the other Soviet-bloc countries, wage differentials are much greater than in Poland. The reason for the squashing of the Polish wage scale is to be sought in the political situation: Since the Party in Poland lacks popularity, it tries to ingratiate itself with the working masses by setting high wage minima and by putting low ceilings on the earnings of skilled personnel. Yet even in Poland, there is an increasing realization that wage differentials are needed to encourage schooling and to serve as a reward for responsibility.

When wage differentials are increased, such increases

[18] *Ibid.*, p. 16.
[19] *Ibid.*, p. 19.

are not always motivated by purely economic considerations. During the period from 1955 to 1957, wage increases were granted in Poland "under a heavy pressure on the part of the working classes ... in this period spontaneous changes often prevailed over planned moves." [20] Wage grants were made to workers threatening revolt and to workers in key jobs (such as mining) who could readily paralyze the economy. Even when the increases were justified by labor market considerations, the amount of increase was often dictated by noneconomic considerations.

It is inherently difficult to pursue a policy of centralized wage planning which would also be a policy consistent with labor market equilibrium. Administered wages may respond to or anticipate the market; in all cases the change involves a guess at the magnitude of the change which would have occurred in a free market. Whenever the guess is incorrect, market disequilibrium follows.

Administered changes take place at discrete time intervals, and they are often slow in coming. The slowness of administered wage responses is caused "by the inherent immobilism of the administrative apparatus and the rigidity of all the major links in the economic apparatus" [21] proper to the soviet-type model. Consequently, when there is urgent need for a wage change, it is usually accomplished through *ad hoc* moves which change relative wages. Such moves usually fail to take into account the impact of the reforms on the entire wage structure.

[20] H. Diamand, *O polityce płac* Warszawa, Książka i Wiedza, 1958, p. 22.

[21] Włodzimierz Brus, *Ogólne problemy funkcjonowania gospodarki socjalistycznej*, Warszawa, Państwowy Instytut Wydawniczy, 1961, p. 130.

When a reform is overdue or when the magnitude of the reform change is miscalculated, the administratively set wages misallocate labor. The economy must accept the misallocation or else it must resort to decentralized adjustments, i.e., to changes in piece-rate payments. Thus centralized wage administration breeds distortions of the base-rate/piece-rate structure, and these distortions in turn impede a rational wage policy.

The multiplicity of goals pursued by the Soviet wage policy inevitably leads to conflicts and compromises. Rewards for individual effort run counter to the use of wages for allocative purposes. The effort to ensure a decent standard to all workers hampers the allocative policy as well as the individual incentive policy. Social considerations in wage setting form a separate criterion from the economic considerations. Where in theory there is social harmony, in practice there are conflicting needs and demands.

The conflicts which exist among the many individual goals and which are reflected in policy goals have received grudging recognition in the recent amendments introduced in the Soviet doctrine. The "contradictions" which arise between "mental and physical labor, qualified and unqualified, heavy and light labor" are duly noted, and so is the "contradiction between the relation of equality with respect to the ownership of the means of production, and the factual inequality in the use of these means of production." [22] Simply speaking, where resources are scarce, one can increase the degree of satisfaction of one goal only at the cost of another. The introduction of the soviet-type system did not eliminate the conflicts; it merely put decision making into the hands of

[22] Y. A. Kronrod, *op. cit.*, pp. 252–262.

the Party leadership and substituted direct allocation for the workings of the market. The Party, in its desire to preserve the workers' freedom of choice, inherited the conflicts which exist under the market mechanism. These conflicts are subdued when the policy is one of elimination of unemployment at all cost. Once unemployment is eliminated, the question of rational use of human resources reappears, and the Party must compromise between rational labor allocation and the application of Marxist and Leninist principles of fair treatment.

The Soviet conception of a harmonious, classless society is not readily reconcilable with the freedom of occupational choice. If workers are to choose their occupations at will, there must be either job creation to suit the workers' liking or wages sufficiently flexible to allocate workers to the available jobs. Planned production excludes the first alternative. The second alternative, complete wage flexibility, runs against the desire to control income distribution and administer wage payments. If wages were left to be determined by supply and demand conditions, the road to wage bargaining would be open. The Communist Party no longer would represent the workers' interests, since the workers would take care of their own. The whole fabric of unitary social structure would collapse.

The concept of a unitary Soviet state leads either to direct labor allocation or to the adoption of makeshift methods whereby supply and demand conditions are approximately reflected by the administered wages. With long practice and administrative improvement, it is possible for the system to work with reasonable efficiency. Even so, the system never succeeds in eliminating the contradictory interests of various groups or workers. Whenever control weakens, as in the period from 1955 to 1957, dissatisfaction erupts and a quasi-rational policy must be abandoned in favor of a policy to please the pressure groups.

b. The Consumers

"The role of the Socialist economy," says a Polish expert on consumption economics, "is not limited to passive adaptation to the tastes and habits of the consumers. The Socialist community as represented by the central planning authorities has its own opinion of the needs of the community which should be fostered and satisfied." [23]

The total bill of consumers' goods, like the total wage bill, is determined by the economic plan. By deciding what product mix to produce and by setting prices at the market clearing level, the policy makers are able to determine the over-all consumption pattern without violating the principle of free consumer choice. For instance, policy makers believe that the consumption of health services is to be encouraged; health services are therefore provided free of charge in all the Soviet-bloc countries. The consumer may, nevertheless, choose not to avail himself of the services if he so desires.

Some departures from the consumers' choice principle which occur in the Soviet-bloc countries are also present in free-enterprise economies. Thus education up to a certain level is compulsory. The educational system differs from that of the West in that (1) the state alone provides education (the Catholic University at Lublin being the sole excep-

[23] Zofia Morecka, *loc. cit.*, p. 489.

tion) and (2) the state frequently applies social criteria in the admission of students.

Another example of departure from the consumer-choice principle is rationing of consumers' goods. Rationing occurs only in times of emergency. It was quite widespread in the Soviet Union in the years following the revolution, and in the other Soviet-bloc countries immediately following the Communist take-over. Some goods (for instance, cars) are still in some cases allotted in accordance with a scheme of priorities. Rationing as a whole is considered an emergency measure to be abandoned as speedily as possible.

The one case of nonmarket allocation which is fundamental to soviet-type policy is rationing of housing space. Unlike the rationing of other consumer goods, housing allotment is a permanent part of the system.

A Polish housing policy expert states why housing is the one exception to the consumers' choice rule adopted by Soviet policy makers:

The aim of the housing policy in a Socialist society is the fullest possible satisfaction of material and cultural existence needs of the working masses. The level of satisfaction of these needs is determined by the economic potentialities of the entire society and not, as under Capitalism, by the opportunities of each individual which are determined by the class to which the individual belongs. . . . The right to an apartment, the right to satisfy one's living needs, becomes, as a consequence of Socialist development, as important a right as the right to work.[24]

[24] Adam Andrzejewski, *Ekonomia gospodarki mieszkaniowej*, Warszawa, Państwowy Instytut Wydawniczy, 1955, pp. 4 and 19.

The "right to a living space" was emphatically asserted by Stalin, who said that it was the duty of the state to provide quarters to all citizens.[25] In practice the Soviet Union and all the Soviet-bloc countries have steadily pursued a policy of below-equilibrium rents and of housing allotments. Such a policy, it is often said, "ensures a fair allotment of housing space to all the citizens." [26]

The rationing of living space serves a multitude of purposes, the most important of which is social equalization. Good living quarters are an overt sign of privilege. Equal housing facilities for all citizens create an impression of social equality and destroy the social character of different areas within a city. Allocation on the basis of need (however defined) rather than wealth is an important step toward the communist principle, "to each according to his needs."

Rationing of living space provides an excellent method of social control. Space is allotted in accordance with a priority scheme designed by the authorities. The housing agencies are subordinate to city Soviets (i.e., city administrations), but various institutions (ministries, enterprises, and even educational and health institutions) have certain housing facilities at their disposal. Thus persons who are of prime importance to the economy or who are politically reliable may be rewarded with good living quarters, while "socially undesirable" individuals are deprived of housing and have to live with relatives or find private quarters—a very costly proposition when rationing is the rule.

Allotments are made on the basis of housing norms. Every

[25] Joseph Stalin, *Problems of Leninism,* Polish edition, Warszawa, 1947, p. 313.

[26] Adam Andrzejewski, *op. cit.,* pp. 33ff.

person is entitled (in theory) to a minimum footage. In addition to the minimum, persons who work at home, who have given meritorious service to the state, or who have "representational" needs may receive extra space. No one is entitled to more than a specified maximum. In practice, many persons live under conditions well below the minimum standard, for the norms represent the leadership's appraisal of minimum needs rather than an appraisal of actual availability.

The double criterion of living-space need and social usefulness of the applicant for space is freely proclaimed by the leadership:

> The authorities which allocate living quarters take into account on one hand the real needs of the citizen and his actual housing situation, and, on the other hand, his usefulness in the fulfillment of the economic tasks of the socialized sector of the economy and in the functioning of the administrative apparatus.[27]

The gradations of social merit are written into the law,[28] but much administrative freedom of action remains.

The proximate reason for rationing of housing space lies in the lower-than-equilibrium rent. Low rents result in an uneconomical use of the existing housing facilities. If rents were set at a level equilibrating supply with demand, many a family would do with less space. The funds now used to

[27] *Ibid.*, p. 186. See also *ibid.*, pp. 187ff.
[28] For Polish housing legislation, see *Dziennik Ustaw Rzeczpospolitej Polskiej*, 1950, no. 36, position 343; 1951, no. 26, position 194; 1952, no. 26, position 196; and *Monitor Polski*, 1951, no. A87, position 1196.

subsidize rents could be utilized for other consumer commodities. It is likely, too, that if higher rents were charged, tenants would value their apartments more; at present there is visible proof that tenants do not pay much attention to the maintenance of their (virtually free) housing.

The low rents which are now being charged prevent adequate maintenance of buildings on the part of the building-owning organizations. It might appear that rent levels do not matter since all rental houses are publicly controlled. In practice the various authorities which own or manage buildings have individual budgets. The lower the rent payments, the greater the burden of maintenance on the budgets. As long as there is a housing shortage and construction budgets are limited, there is a clear preference for the erection of new buildings over the maintenance of old ones.

The insufficiency of rent payments for maintenance purposes may be illustrated by a Polish example. In 1958 rent payments for apartments in Polish cities amounted to 1.7 billion złotys. The actual maintenance expenditures (which were substantially lower than the maintenance needs) equalled 4.8 billion złotys.[29]

The continuing need for rationing stems from the unwillingness or inability of the state to provide sufficient housing at the rents fixed by the state itself. Contrary to Stalin's dicta, very low priorities are assigned to housing expenditure. Even in Poland, where the housing shortage was especially acute as a consequence of war devastation,

[29] Wiktor Nieciemski, "Gospodarka mieszkaniowa," *Rocznik polityczny i gospodarczy, 1959*, Warszawa, Polskie Wydawnictwa Gospodarcze, 1960, p. 635.

housing construction failed to keep up with population growth during the Stalinist period.

Table 3   Housing conditions in Poland, 1950–1955

	1950	1955
Population	25,000,000	27,500,000
Total number of rooms	13,670,000	14,155,000
Persons per room: country as a whole	1.83	1.94
Persons per room: urban areas	1.54	1.77
Persons per room: rural areas	2.05	2.10

Source: Stanisław Wyrobisz, *Studia i rozważania o rozwoju gospodarczym Polski*, Warszawa, Książka i Wiedza, 1959, p. 94.

The reasons for the neglect of housing are not hard to find. Construction materials are needed for the erection of new manufacturing facilities which receive high priority.[30] Only when public pressure forces the relaxation of the tempo of investment is housing permitted to expand. Thus after the 1956 Polish "revolution," authorities took steps to improve the housing situation. These steps represent a clear retreat from the basic policy principle. Hence, one may

[30] In 1937, 82 per cent of the cubic space of new construction was devoted to housing, and 18 per cent to industrial and commercial uses. In 1955, housing space amounted to 40 per cent and industrial and commercial construction to 60 per cent of the cubic space. (See Jerzy Bogusz, *Zasady nowej polityki mieszkaniowej*, Warszawa, Książka i Wiedza, 1959, p. 5.) It must be noted that in the interwar period industrial and commercial construction in Poland proceeded at a slow pace. However, a similar lag in housing construction compared with the prewar rate and compared to all the major free-enterprise countries is noted throughout the Soviet camp.

assume that they will be rescinded when the situation is eased.

Under the post-1956 Polish policy, housing is no longer allotted solely in recognition of personal needs and social merit, but differentiation according to the economic resources of the individual is also permitted. A person may not be especially meritorious according to the policy makers' criteria, but if he has private means, he can get better housing and get it faster than a person in worse economic circumstances.

In Poland since 1956 there have been two kinds of housing cooperatives, as well as privately owned single-family dwelling units. The cheapest housing is provided by so-called "tenant cooperatives," which receive the highest government subsidy.[31] Apartments are allocated in the tenant cooperatives in accordance with housing norms, and members of the cooperative are co-owners of the entire building and not owners of individual apartments. When the family of a tenant expands, he is entitled to a larger apartment, and when the family unit diminishes in size, the tenant must give up his apartment for a smaller one.

The tenant-type cooperatives are frequently attached to individual enterprises which, since 1956, have disposed of some housing construction funds which can be used at their own discretion. To the tenants, the cooperatives provide somewhat better housing than allotments at somewhat

[31] The subsidy system takes the form of initial credits and of outright government gifts. If the credit is repaid at a stated rate, part of it is transformed into another gift. Repayment at a faster rate results in an even greater outright subsidy. The subsidy may be diminished or even cancelled if the cooperative fails to conform to the allotment norms, or if facilities are poorly maintained. (See J. Bogusz, *op. cit.*, pp. 16–22.)

higher cost, but the main advantage lies in the speed with which the allotments can be made.

The owner-type cooperatives also receive a government subsidy, but a smaller one than the tenant-type. In these co-operatives, each member becomes the owner of an apart-ment. Though there are set square footage maxima, they are substantially more liberal than in the other types of housing. The owner-type cooperative apartments are more expensive than the tenant-type, but the advantages to the members are quite evident.

Individual housing is the least desirable from the point of view of Soviet policy makers. Such housing harks back to the "bourgeois society," and also (it is claimed) [32] uses up more raw materials. Nevertheless, when housing shortage was at its most acute and dissatisfaction was rife, the gov-ernment of Poland not only tolerated private construction but encouraged it through credits.

The relaxation of the housing policy in Poland does not signify abdication of social control. The government remains all powerful, and at any time it may modify or even reverse its policy. In 1962, private housing was much more restricted than it had been a few years previously. It is readily con-ceivable that it will be entirely eliminated in the future.

The Polish housing policy is an example of the pragmatic approach prevalent in the post-Stalinist period. A retreat from a set social policy takes place when the policy proves too costly economically. Such a retreat should not be mis-taken for a change in avowed goals, which remain much the same as in the previous period.

Through its housing policy the Party controls where the citizens will live. The educational policy gives the Party a

[32] *Ibid.*, p. 23.

measure of control over the selection of future leaders. Yet in the vast majority of decisions, the individual is free to choose what he will do and what he will purchase. Thus, in theory, a vast area of consumer choice is preserved, though in practice, persistent shortages often lead to nonprice allocation.

Until the middle 1950s, consumer choice was hampered in all the Soviet-bloc countries by a persistent suppressed inflation. Aggregate wage payments rose faster than the supply of consumer goods, while prices were kept down. This phenomenon was justified in terms of a "law" which stated that under socialism, consumer demand must "propel forward" consumption and be an incentive to increase production.[33] Whether the theory influenced the practice or whether practice was given an ex post facto theoretical stamp of approval is difficult to say. One suspects that the lag of consumer goods behind purchasing power was the result of laxity in wage payments policy and nonfulfillment of consumer goods plans.[34] Since mistakes are unthinkable in a planned economy, the theory was evolved as a cover-up.

Under conditions of hidden inflation, the degree of consumer control over the product mix is extremely weak. Whatever goods happen to be available are purchased. When virtually all goods are in short supply, there is an appearance of urgent need for all commodities. Mistakes in

[33] See J. Stalin's pronouncements at the 16th Congress of the RCP. (Source: J. Stalin, *Works*, Polish edition, Warszawa, Książka i Wiedza, 1951, p. 293 and pp. 322–323.)

[34] It is well known that consumers goods production is often sacrificed when the plans prove too ambitious.

assortment planning remain hidden since all goods find a ready market.

A policy of suppressed inflation proves unsatisfactory in the long run to the consumers as well as to the planners. The consumers are condemned to long waits in queues and constantly run against shortages. Suppressed inflation encourages black market operations which redistribute income and withdraw certain individuals from the state's productive machine. Finally, when all goods find a purchaser, quality control is exceedingly difficult and resources are dissipated in shoddy production.

In recent years, all soviet-type economies have adopted a policy of retail market equilibrium. The over-all demand is matched by an over-all supply, and efforts are made to equate the supply and demand of every good. In planning production, provision is made to accumulate consumer goods inventories to ensure continuity of supply of all goods.

The policy of equilibrium and inventory accumulation was accepted with misgivings. Thus the Polish Economic Council (an advisory body which includes non-Marxist economists) stated that:

To ensure partial equilibrium in a developing economy is a particularly difficult task because even the formation of certain inventories (which is equivalent to a slowing down of the consumption rate) can fail as an equilibrating device because of the difficulty in forecasting the development of consumer demand.[35]

[35] Rada Ekonomiczna przy Radzie Ministrów, *Sytuacja gospodarcza kraju w roku 1959*, Warszawa, Polskie Wydawnictwa Gospodarcze, 1960, p. 7.

This quotation illustrates the two common objections to the policy of equilibrating supply and demand for consumer goods through inventory holdings. The first objection is that inventory holdings represent consumption delay. A policy of suppressed inflation would permit the consumption of goods which are accumulated as inventories under a policy of partial equilibrium. When needs are urgent (that is, when the consumer goods bill is small), the carrying of consumer inventories may represent a considerable burden. This burden must be measured against the convenience of regularity of supply—a factor which does not seem to receive much attention in the Soviet economies.

The policy of equilibrium through inventories may be effective when inventories serve to smooth out an uneven demand (or uneven supply stream) of known aggregate magnitude. The demand for certain types of clothing is highly seasonal while production may be distributed more evenly throughout the year. If the aggregate demand in the peak season is known, it is possible to calculate the proper size of inventories to accommodate demand. When the magnitude of demand is not known, the inventory policy is likely to fail. It is clear that consumer demand is more difficult to predict in an economy which evolves rapidly than in a static one. Consequently, a policy of matching supply and demand cannot be based on inventory accumulation alone, but must also resort to price and/or supply flexibility. Both devices are used though neither to a sufficient extent.

The use of price mechanism to ensure partial equilibrium in the consumer goods market is now accepted *in principle* in the soviet-type economies. The reliance on flexible pricing does not indicate in any way that the state has abandoned its prerogative of dictating to the consumers what they should purchase:

> The system of retail prices should be adjusted so as to ensure market equilibrium. Prices should mold demand in order to equate actual consumption with the consumption pattern foreseen by the plan.[36]

In other words, the policy makers decide what goods should be consumed and this decision determines the supply pattern. The price system is merely a device for equating actual demand with the planned supply. In practice, as we shall see, consumer preferences do have an influence on the consumer goods bill, but in theory, the policy makers retain full control and resort to pricing as a policy tool.

The use of administered prices as a device for equating supply and demand poses two requirements: First, the administrators must have a precise knowledge of the demand conditions (and also of supply conditions, if supply responds to price) and second, the system must permit frequent adjustments to correct possible mistakes. Neither requirement is satisfied in practice.

Under a regime of administered prices, a shortage indicates that the price of the good in short supply is too low, while a surplus indicates that the price is too high. The amount of the surplus is easily calculated, provided inventory reporting is well organized. The magnitude of a shortage is much more difficult to appraise. The only indication of the magnitude of a shortage, albeit a very im-

[36] Bronisław Minc, "Zagadniena wyboru ekonomicznego w planowaniu oraz problemy cen," in O. Lange (ed.), *op. cit.*, p. 368.

perfect one, is given by the price established in the black market. Even so, when there is a suppressed inflation, it is almost impossible to calculate the relative deficits of the various categories of goods.

To calculate the magnitude of the price adjustment needed to restore equilibrium, it is essential to know the elasticity of demand and the magnitude of demand response to price changes. Some modest beginnings of calculations based on consumer budget studies have been made in recent years, but such calculations are too sporadic to dispel the general ignorance.[37]

In countries such as Poland, where income differentials are very small, the use of prices as an equilibrating device is particularly difficult. At one price a given good is inaccessible to the vast majority of the population. A relatively small price cut puts it within the range of the low-income worker. Such "demand avalanches" have been observed in the case of many consumer durables, such as radios, motorcycles, and television sets. The shock of a demand avalanche is lessened occasionally through imports of consumer goods in short supply. Thus the policy of equilibrating through the price mechanism is supplemented by a policy of flexible supplies. Since domestic planning leaves no room for flexibility, the foreign market must be used for aid.[37a]

---

[37] For a discussion of the application of consumer budget studies to planning in Czechoslovakia, see Jan Bezouszka, "Wykorzystanie statystyki budżetów rodzinnych do pełnego poznania spożycia indywidualnego w Czechosłowacji," *Wiadomości Statystyczne*, vol. 5, no. 2, March–April, 1960.

[37a] See Rada Ekonomiczna przy Radzie Ministrów, *op. cit.*, p. 367.

Ignorance of the magnitude of demand responses to price changes leads to a policy of immobilism. This policy is also encouraged by ignorance of the side effects accompanying price changes. A price cut increases not only the demand for the good affected by the cut, but also the demand for complementary goods, while it diminishes the demand for competitive goods. If the demand for the good affected by the price cut is elastic, the aggregate demand for all other goods diminishes; if it is inelastic, the aggregate demand increases. Thus a price change cannot be looked upon in isolation, especially if the commodity plays an important role in the consumer budget. Since the interconnections are veiled by a most profound ignorance, price-setting authorities prefer to leave well enough alone for fear of disturbing the equilibrium of other goods.

The immobilism of the price-setting authorities is also fostered by the magnitude of the task. All the prices in a soviet-type economy (excluding some of the prices of goods and services provided by the private sector) are set by central authority. With tens of thousands of prices to set, price-setting authorities ignore the less irksome disequilibria and concentrate on the points which call for most urgent reform.[38]

When price changes are made they usually take the form of major "reforms." As one Polish authority on consumer economics put it, "it is characteristic of the Socialist economy

[38] The magnitude of the task of price setting may be best perceived by perusing the official price bulletins. In Poland a basic price list of retail goods was established in May, 1954, and was still in force in 1960 except as amended. The amendments are quite numerous. For instance, in 1959, ninety-eight prices

that the variables which influence market equilibrium and which are under the direct control of the state move in discontinuous jumps." [39]

The dual tendency toward price immobilism and discontinuous changes may be illustrated by looking at consumer price behavior from 1955 to 1959. Between the two dates, Poland underwent major political and economic upheavals. Yet the average price of fifteen important consumer goods (out of a total of forty-eight) remained invariant throughout the period. The average price of another seventeen commodities changed by 20 per cent or more—some changes surpassing 100 per cent. Only seventeen commodities changed by less than 20 per cent, and most of these small changes were token reductions in price made for propaganda purposes in the face of a general price rise. [40]

It is one of the paradoxes of the soviet-type system that the consumers reinforce the immobilism of the price mechanism. Consumers have a vested interest in not permitting prices to rise. When prices are administratively determined, consumers exert pressure on the administration to keep

---

were announced for different grades of boys' shirts and over fifty prices of boys' suits. Such amendments come in waves; a change in one price requires changes in other prices as well. It is reported that a single price change involves several hundred pages of form-filling and calculations. A policy of no change saves much work and prevents potential miscalculations.

[39] K. Boczar, *Społeczno-gospodarcze podstawy obrotu towarowego*, Warszawa, Książka i Wiedza, 1960, p. 78.

[40] Source of data: Central Statistical Office, quoted by W. Gomułka, *Aktualne trudności na rynku mięsnym i środki niezbędne dla ich przezwyciężenia*, Warszawa, Książka i Wiedza, 1959, pp. 16–18.

prices down. This phenomenon is familiar in the West as well as in the soviet-type economies: Where there are rent controls, pressure builds up against any revision of the control level. Similarly, public services such as municipal transport must constantly battle the public to permit increases in charges.

In an economy in which virtually all prices are set by administrative action, any upward revision of prices becomes a matter of public concern. To diminish public opposition to price changes, a policy of matched changes is generally pursued. When the price of a commodity has to be increased, efforts are made to cut other prices to leave real income on approximately the same level as before the change.

When there is a market disequilibrium in an important category of products and where there is no possibility of compensating changes, political leadership may resort to an "acute crisis" device. The price change is represented as a national necessity and heralded by a long educational campaign. Such was the case in the Polish 1959 meat crisis. The "crisis" was caused by long-term immobility in meat prices in a period of rising money incomes and rising agricultural production costs. Since meat is produced in Poland primarily by private farmers, the meat supply shrank as feed costs rose. Simultaneously a fast rise in nominal wages, unmatched by a corresponding increase in the availability of consumer goods, increased the demand for meat.

The increase in meat prices was an event of such general importance that it had to be taken up as a major item by the 3d Plenum of the Central Committee of the Party. The meeting was preceded by a lengthy press campaign which presented in striking terms the necessity of cutting down consumption for the sake of plan fulfillment. The culminating point was a lengthy speech by Gomułka who personally announced the changes. Prices of meat went up at a stroke by 25 per cent. The price of pork (the most important meat) increased by 28 per cent.[41] These radical changes took place after years of price stability, and they heralded another long period of stable prices.

The difficulty of changing product prices leads to a policy of equilibrating supply and demand by manipulating quantities supplied. In the annual reports of the Polish Economic Council attached to the Cabinet, we repeatedly read about the "shortage" of certain goods and the "insufficiency" of inventories to satisfy the needs of trade.[42] There is no suggestion that the prices should be adjusted; on the contrary, the Council's recommendations deal with the level of production of the various commodities. In some cases these recommendations are based on an estimate of the "proper" supply levels, but more often they are based on the observation of surpluses or shortages prevailing at the existing price. Since many consumer goods prices bear no relation to costs but are determined by historical precedent, the achievement of market equilibrium through supply adjustment often leads to absurd consequences: The quantity of certain goods is dictated neither by consumer preferences nor by policy makers' preferences, but by the ruling price.

[41] Gomułka, *ibid.*, p. 41.

[42] Rada Ekonomiczna przy Radzie Ministrów, *Główne problemy gospodarcze kraju w roku 1957*, Warszawa, Polskie Wydawnictwa Gospodarcze, 1958, p. 129.

The maintenance of quasi-complete sovereignty in the hands of the policy makers is incompatible with consumer dictation of aggregate wishes. It is of great importance to the system that sovereignty be maintained in the hands of the Party. It is also important, however, that there be no overt conflict between the Party and the consumers. If the Party is to represent the true interests of the consumers, it may overrule the consumers' aggregate wishes, if such wishes are molded by an improper ideological stand of the people. Thus the Party may rule against abstract art, popular music, or other "corrupting" goods and services. It would be patently absurd for the Party to dictate that people should prefer one pattern of shirt material to another. In all such "neutral" issues, attempts are made to follow consumer preferences.

The consumers' control over the assortment of consumer goods increased markedly from the middle 1950s. With the disappearance of suppressed inflation, consumer buying became more selective. Simultaneously, a series of reforms increased the producers' responsiveness to the consumers' selection. Thus, in Poland, retail outlets received the right to choose their own suppliers and also to reject unwanted merchandise. The quality of retail service was improved by a new method of granting premiums. Under the old system, each employee was paid according to the volume of his individual sales. The resulting tendency was to minimize the number of sales clerks in order to increase each clerk's pay. The policy was dictated by the desire to minimize the "unproductive" employment in trade. With the recognition of the importance of decent service to the consumers came a method of group premiums based on the total volume of sales of a store. Under this system each store became interested in maximizing total sales,[43] and therefore, in the salability of the merchandise.[44]

Changes in retailing methods brought some improvement in the quality and type of consumer goods. There remained, however, the broader questions of goods assortment and the network of retail markets. The locations and types of stores are determined in the soviet-type economies through a rather haphazard method—a mixture of common sense and copying the free-enterprise pattern, modified by the deep conviction that too many retail outlets are a harmful thing. To some extent, public clamor for stores is heeded. When the inhabitants of a given area persist in their demands for a specific type of store, they may be granted their wish. The advisability of maintaining existing stores is reckoned through profitability calculations. A store which fails to meet minimum requirements is likely to be converted or discontinued.

No practical schemes for reckoning the intensity of need for retail markets has been proposed as yet. A Polish economist, A. Wakar, suggested that a sort of Gallup poll be held every so often to determine how much the inhabitants of a given region would be willing to pay in exchange for improvements in service. Wakar claims that such a poll would be a highly scientific method of measuring the in-

[43] The number of sales personnel remains limited because each store has a wage plan. Under the old system, there was a tendency to hire fewer persons than permitted by the plan.

[44] Piotr Jaroszewicz, Inaugural Address, in *Handel Wewnętrzny,* vol. 5 (January–March, 1959), pp. 10ff.

tensity of consumer needs and that the method would be especially appropriate in socialist economics.[45]

Wakar's proposal has not yet been translated into practice. At best it gives a rather imperfect picture of probable market demand. Unless the expressed desires are weighted by the magnitude of probable expenditures, there is no way of knowing whether the proposed retail outlet is really needed or not. There is also a great potential gap between an expression of interest in a new retail store and actual purchases.

Attempts to improve the quality of consumer goods have led to the introduction of brand names. Brands which consumers dislike accumulate on the retailers' shelves. The retailers are materially interested in fulfilling their plan which sets over-all sales quotas; hence they are unlikely to reorder products which are difficult to sell. The manufacturer, also interested in plan fulfillment, must either improve the product or change his assortment—which, within limits, he is permitted to do. Thus the consumer can influence the quality of the product and, to a limited extent, the product mix.

To prevent the accumulation of inventories of unpopular or defective products, retailers are now permitted to hold reduced-price sales. For retail business as a whole, reductions may amount to 0.5 per cent of the turnover. For example, a branch which sells 1 million złotys worth of goods per month at an average price of 100 złotys per unit is permitted to "lose" 5,000 złotys per month by selling, say, an additional 80 units at an average price of 62.50 złotys.

[45] A. Wakar, "Zagadnienie teorii handlu socjalistycznego," *ibid.*, pp. 6ff.

Reduced-price sales are preferable from the retailers' point of view to inventory accumulation, but they are not equivalent to full-price sales. The reduced-price sales thus benefit the consumers without eliminating the influence of consumers' choice on production.[46]

It is all too easy to exaggerate the strength of consumers' influence on the product mix. The influence is limited to minor assortment decisions and quality changes. When a given model of radio is unpopular, the manufacturer may switch to a more popular model provided both models are included in the manufacturer's plan. The system does not permit consumers to influence resource allocation away from radios and in favor of, say, motorcycles. Indeed, consumer reluctance to buy radios is likely to lead (after a lapse of time) to the lowering of radio prices. If at the lower price a shortage of radios develops, it is conceivable that radio production will be adjusted upward. Thus in the absence of prices based on costs and the profit motive, the consumer goods price mechanism may act in a perverse fashion.[47]

The difficulty of satisfying keenly felt consumer wishes leads to the familiar phenomenon of so-called "façade building." Façade building is a token expression of the concern of the Party leadership for consumer welfare. One of the most common manifestations of façade building is the

[46] See Rada Ekonomiczna przy Radzie Ministrów, *Sytuacja ekonomiczna kraju w roku 1958*, Warszawa, Polskie Wydawnictwa Gospodarcze, 1959, p. 159.

[47] There is a limit to this process: Under current ground rules the price of the product must cover "production costs." Since virtually all consumer goods prices carry a wide margin over and above the "costs," the floor is not very effective. For a discussion of the definition of "production costs" see Chap. 5 below.

display in special "sample stores" of goods which are not yet in production but which (at an unspecified date) will become available. The construction of "model homes" is another example. Through façade building the policy makers express their concern for consumer welfare by showing what the consumers will receive when circumstances permit. Whether the device of façade building actually achieves its purpose is much open to doubt. Too many unfulfilled promises lead to frustration and a general feeling of being fooled; too much façade building leads to discouragement rather than to greater and greater productive effort.

The policy toward the consumer defies a simple summation. The policy makers want to retain decision making in their own hands, but wish to avoid any overt conflict with the consumers' wishes. If the consumers were truly free to choose the goods they wish, that is, if the retail market were in balance, there would be no reason for overt conflict. In practice, the maintenance of equilibrium through administrative action proves exceedingly difficult. Moreover, the system of granting goods and fixing prices by central authority breeds an attitude among consumers that they may make demands on the policy makers. Since the policy makers are free to decide what will be produced and how goods will be priced, the consumers exert constant pressure for more and cheaper goods. When sacrifice is divorced from reward, each consumer wants more for less. The unitary, harmonious society remains a myth; conflicts between producers and consumers are replaced by a conflict between consumers and the all-powerful authority which doles out consumer goods.

4

Long-term and
Perspective Plans

a. Scope and Purpose of Long-term Planning

Soviet-type economies are governed by a hierarchy of plans. The national plans range from perspective plans (ten years or more) through long-range (three to seven years) to annual plans. The activity of regions, industries, enterprises, and scientific institutes is also mapped out in plans. Most of the sectional plans cover periods of one year or less (quarterly enterprise plans are quite common), though recent years saw the development of multiyear plans for enterprises and research teams.

Broad reforms and major development goals appear with clarity in the long-range and perspective plans only:

A multiyear plan can, and often should, introduce basic changes in the national economy compared with the previous period. Over the annual plan period, it is extremely difficult to introduce basic reforms.[1]

In the short run—and in economic development a year is a very short period—the character of the economy is fixed. Even an intensive drive requires years to transform an agricultural country into an industrial one or to retool industry from consumer goods to producer goods. The annual changes are marginal, and only their cumulation transforms the economy. Long-term and perspective plans depict the direction and the magnitude of these cumulative effects.

Long-term and perspective plans provide a framework for short-term plans, but are not themselves operational documents:

> The character and magnitude of development of the individual branches of the economy in the long-term plan period are not as clearly determined as in the annual plan. This is because the development in the long-term period is determined by elements which do not as yet exist, and which are yet to occur.[2]

The long-term plan (and even more so the perspective plan) gives a broad sweep of development, but few specific details. The operational plans valid for one-year periods are detailed blueprints for action. Each operational plan must take into account the economy's position at the beginning of the planning period and the desired direction of change.

[1] Mieczysław Rakowski, *Zagadnienia planowania wieloletniego w Polsce Ludowej*, Warszawa, Polskie Wydawnictwa Gospodarcze, 1955, p. 26.

[2] *Ibid.*, p. 6.

The long-term plan is not concerned with details, but with over-all policy. As time passes and unforeseen developments occur, the long-term plan is of less and less importance, and short-term documents are based more on *ad hoc* Party directives than on the long-term documents. The latter are sometimes scrapped; quite often they are merely disregarded.

Each long-term plan concentrates on a set of primary economic and social objectives around which the plan is structured and which serve as slogans. For instance, Poland's Three-Year Plan (1947 to 1949) was aimed at the reconstruction of war damage, at the nationalization of all the important industries, and at land reform. Toward the end of the plan, the Soviet camp adopted a hard policy of rapid expansion, armament, and tightening of the Communist hold. Poland's economy, along with the economies of the other satellite nations, had to be geared to the new program and the development of heavy industry was accelerated beyond the planned tempo.[3]

The Six-Year Plan covering the years 1950 to 1955 reflects the new policy:

The basic task of the plan is the construction of socialism in Poland. . . . Small enterprise [which at the time was not nationalized] is the source of growth of capitalism and it is necessary to transform the small enterprise economy into a socialist

[3] The early days of planning in the so-called "popular democracies" and the interconnection between economic plans and political objectives are described in detail in an excellent study by Jan Marczewski. See his *Planification et croissance économique des démocraties populaires,* Paris, Presses Universitaires de France, 1956.

economy. To accomplish this task we must first achieve the necessary raw material and technological basis, which can only be accomplished through the development of capital goods industries.[4]

The Six-Year Plan undertook to transform Poland from a primarily agricultural country to one in which industry and agriculture stood at par. Under the plan's original premises industrial output was to grow 11 to 12 per cent per year—a high, but feasible goal. The main emphasis was put on the iron and steel industry, which was supposed to double its output, and on heavy mechanical industries.[5]

Soon after its inception, the Six-Year Plan—as well as the plans of all the other nations in the Soviet sphere—was sharply revised upwards under direct pressure from the Soviet Union. In Poland the goal of an 11 per cent annual increase in industrial production was boosted to 17 per cent, with the major effort directed at heavy industry and armaments. The most extreme revision was made in the Hungarian plan, where the goal of 13 per cent was exactly doubled.[6] The change in objectives transformed the plans into crash programs of armaments and of heavy industrial construction.

The Polish Six-Year Plan (and the corresponding plans of the other countries of the Camp) concentrated on a few objectives with almost total disregard of costs. The results

[4] Hilary Minc, Report to the Congress of the Polish United Workers' Party, Dec. 18, 1948, printed as Hilary Minc, *Osiągnięcia i plany gospodarcze*, Warszawa, Książka i Wiedza, 1949, p. 63.

[5] *Ibid.*, pp. 65ff.

[6] See Jan Marczewski, *op. cit.*, vol. 1, pp. 187ff.

of the plan are difficult to gauge, since the period is characterized by paucity of statistical data and an extreme unreliability of published figures. There is no doubt that industrial output rose for the period as a whole, especially the output of heavy industry. In Poland a substantial proportion of the increase is attributable to the growth of industrial employment which rose (in the nationalized sector) from 1.7 to 2.7 million workers between 1949 and 1955.[7] Output increases were also achieved through improved management of former German properties, many of which were far from being well utilized at the beginning of the plan. New investments contributed relatively little; 76 per cent of the expansion in output was obtained from existing facilities and another 14 per cent from the enlargement of old factories. New plants contributed only 10 per cent of the growth.[8] This figure is extremely low if one considers that as of 1955, 38 per cent of total industrial capital in Poland was of postwar vintage, and most of it was built under the Six-Year Plan.[9] Most of the projects undertaken under the plan were not finished by the end of the period, and those which were had typical "infant industry" troubles.

Official performance figures show a rise of 174 per cent in the output of nationalized industry for the period as a whole. These results (which probably should not be taken

[7] Główny Urząd Statystyczny, *Rocznik statystyczny*, 1959.

[8] Eugeniusz Szyr, *Niektóre problemy rozwoju gospodarki narodowej w latach 1959–1965*, Warszawa, Książka i Wiedza, 1959, p. 22.

[9] Komisja Planowania przy Radzie Ministrów (information given verbally).

at their face value) were achieved at the cost of decapitalization of industry and agriculture and at the cost of living standards. In industry, maintenance and replacement expenditures averaged somewhat more than 1 per cent of the estimated reproduction cost of fixed capital; in agriculture less than 0.5 per cent.[10] In coal mining, output per man-day fell by 7.7 per cent while the length of the workday was increased.[11] In other industries productivity rose, but the quality of the product deteriorated. Agricultural output increased slightly, because there was an increase in acreage of cultivated land in former German territories, but forced deliveries at low prices and a strong collectivization drive slowed down the recovery of this important sector of the economy.

Consumers suffered chiefly through the deterioration of housing conditions, for new construction did not keep pace with the rising population. Nationalized industry expanded the output of consumer goods, but the private sector was virtually suppressed. During the Six-Year Plan the output of artisans and small private businesses (which produced mainly consumer goods) fell by 75 per cent, and private retail trade shrank by 82 per cent. Whether on balance consumers were better or worse off is difficult to determine, but in any case it is certain that the living standards did not rise rapidly.

The ambitious program mapped out by the Six-Year Plan could be carried out only under conditions of extreme po-

[10] *Ibid.*
[11] *Ibid.* See also W. Gomułka, *Address to the 8th Plenary Session of the Central Committee of the Polish United Workers' Party,* Warsaw, Polonia Publishing House, 1956, pp. 5ff.

litical pressure. When the Party's grip on the country loosened after Stalin's death, the program had to be revised. In 1954 it was decided to freeze investments at the 1953 level and to devote output increases to the improvement of wages.[12] Looking at the period from 1949 to 1956 as a whole, only 62 per cent of the planned investments were executed, and the cost of the investments was much higher than originally estimated.

The next plan, from 1956 to 1960, set as its only "inviolable goal" a 30 per cent increase in real wages.[13] The preamble to the plan states that its purpose is:

... to raise real wages in the cities and income in the countryside; to remove, or at least mitigate, economic disproportions, guaranteeing a more harmonious development.

The measures undertaken in this respect consisted, first of all, of a deemphasis on investment and the allotment of a larger share of production to consumer goods. During the Six-Year Plan, investment growth outpaced by far the growth of consumer goods. This is apparent even from official figures, and there is strong reason to believe that these figures enormously exaggerate the increase in consumer goods production. By contrast, the Five-Year Plan foresaw a development of consumption and investment at approximately equal pace. Table 4 shows the official production growth indices for the Six-Year Plan period and the planned production indices for the subsequent Five-Year Plan.

[12] K. Secomski, *Premises of the Five Year Plan in Poland 1956–1961*, Warsaw, Polonia Publishing House, 1958, p. 18.
[13] *Ibid.*, p. 21.

Table 4   *Growth of consumer goods production and of investment goods production during the Six-Year Plan of
Poland (1949–1955) and growth of production
planned for the Five-Year Plan (1956–1961)*

	1955 output index (actual, 1949 = 100)	1961 output index (planned, 1955 = 100)
Consumer goods	163	146
Investment goods	252	142

Source of data: K. Secomski, *Premises of the Five Year Plan in Poland 1956–1961,* Warsaw, Polonia Publishing House, 1958, pp. 15 and 26.

The structure of investment expenditure, as shown in Table 5, indicates a switch from industry, defense, and administration to an increased emphasis on housing and agriculture.

The new emphasis on consumer goods was accompanied by a relaxation of the policy of suppression of private enterprise. Individual farms and (to a lesser extent) private artisans were to be tolerated once again. Consequently, investment in the private sector, which equaled only 7 per cent of total investment in 1955, was allowed to rise to 15 per cent of the total by 1960.

Most of the investments undertaken from 1956 to 1960 were remedial operations to finish uncompleted projects or to provide "missing links" in the productive patterns. Only 25 per cent of the investment funds were destined for new projects and 75 per cent went for the completion of projects started during the Six-Year Plan.[14] Heavy industrial in-

[14] These figures are based on an analysis of major investment projects which account for 50 per cent of the investment

Table 5 *Composition of Poland's investment expenditures,*
1951–1955 and 1956–1960

	Percentage of total investment	
	1951–1955 (actual)	1956–1960 (planned)
Productive expenditures		
Industry	45	40
Agriculture and forestry	13	19
Building	2	3
Transport and communication	12	9
Nonproductive expenditures		
Housing	12	16
Municipal economy	2	3
Social and cultural facilities	5	6
Defense and administration	6	2
Others	3	3

Note: Because of rounding errors, the percentages do not add up to 100.

Source: K. Secomski, *Premises of the Five Year Plan in Poland 1956–1961*, Warsaw, Polonia Publishing House, 1958, p. 70.

vestments were concentrated in the electric energy field and in the construction materials industry. These two industries were neglected in the previous period and, as a consequence, industrial production was slowed down through power cuts and construction was delayed by building material shortages.

The plan for 1956 to 1960 foresaw two distinct periods. In the first the plan concentrated on increases in real wages and the rectification of mistakes made under the previous

planned for the period. Source: Rada Ekonomiczna przy Radzie Ministrów, *Przegląd bieżącej sytuacji gospodarczej kraju*, Warszawa, Polskie Wydawnictwa Gospodarcze, 1957, pp. 29–33.

plan. In the last two years of the plan, there was to be a resumption of industrial expansion. As it happened, the division between the two stages was much sharper than planned.

In 1957, only a year after its inception, the plan was revised downward. In the revision the 1960 goals for industry were cut by some 4 per cent; the major cut was made in the producer goods sector, where goals were lowered by almost 14 per cent. Consumer goods production programs, on the other hand, were increased by almost 2 per cent.

Two years later, there came a revision in the opposite direction. New goals were outlined by the Party leadership at the 3d Party Congress held in March, 1959:

> The next seven years are a new, higher stage in the Socialist industrialization of Poland. . . . Following the current stage of smoothing out the disproportions which arose in the past, this new stage requires a greater effort and the use of greater means in the development of the branches of industry which have a basic importance for the development of the whole economy, that is, on the production of means of production. At the same time we should not neglect those branches of industry which produce goods to satisfy the needs of the population.[15]

Directives for a new Five-Year Plan covering the years from 1961 to 1965 were adopted at the 3d Party Congress in March, 1959. The directives show a partial return to the fast industrialization policy, though not in such an extreme form as during the Six-Year Plan. A year later, in June,

[15] Stefan Jędrychowski, "Wytyczne rozwoju gospodarki narodowej w latach 1959–1965," *III zjazd PZPR*, Warszawa, Kziążka i Wiedza, 1959, p. 341.

1960, a new set of directives was adopted at the 5th Plenum of the Party's Central Committee. Though ostensibly increasing all the goals—including consumer goods production—the Plenum decided to sacrifice some consumer goods output to achieve quicker industrialization.

The policy changes which occurred from 1959 to 1960 were motivated by political as well as economic factors. The economic reason for the acceleration of investment was, first and foremost, motivated by the desire to maintain full employment. The 1956 to 1960 readjustment period coincided with a demographic trough: During that period the number of new entrants into the labor force fluctuated around 400,000 per year. By contrast, it was expected that the 1962 entrants will number 531,000 and the 1965 entrants over 600,000.[16] To provide jobs for those workers, the investment toward the end of the 1956 to 1960 period was planned at a higher level than at the beginning.

Political motives, too, influenced the planned rate of investment:

> In determining the goals of economic development for the years 1959 to 65, we consider the internal situation of our country in the first place. We also take into account the international balance of force.[17]

In this respect, the lead is taken from the Soviet Union, which sets the investment pace for the other nations of the bloc. The Soviet Union aimed to surpass the United States production level by 1970. Poland was to have a more

[16] K. Secomski, *op. cit.*, p. 77.
[17] Eugeniusz Szyr, *op. cit.*, p. 17.

modest goal, but it was to grow at the pace indicated by its great neighbor.[18]

The mixture of economic and political considerations which determines the over-all proportions set out by the successive plans (and by the modifying directives) also influences the choice of individual investment projects. During the Six-Year Plan, great steel works were constructed near Cracow and Warsaw to strengthen the proletarian character of the two cities. Since every advanced industrialized country has an automobile industry, a large automobile plant was built in Poland. The plant, according to Gomułka, "at incommensurably high production costs turns out an insignificant number of motor cars that consume a lot of petrol, an obsolete model of a kind probably no longer produced anywhere in the world." [19] Recent years have witnessed an increased emphasis on economic analysis, but political considerations continue to play a large role in the selection of individual projects as well as in the determination of the over-all pattern of development.

A bird's-eye view of Poland's postwar plans gives an impression of continuous shifts and changes. Every plan went through several initial versions and had to be changed in the course of execution. The same holds true for the plans of the other Soviet-bloc countries. Such changes are inevitable. A long-range plan is a technical document requiring a year or more of preparatory work. The 1961 to 1965 plan, for instance, was initially based on directives issued in 1958 which, in turn, relied on 1957 statistics. In the interim,

[18] *Ibid.*, pp. 18ff.
[19] W. Gomułka, *Address to the 8th Plenary Session*, p. 5.

between 1957 and 1961, the economy changed and progressed, and social and political circumstances were altered. Even the final document cannot foresee future changes, and therefore it is more than likely that the current plan will be modified before the end of the planned period.

What, then, is the purpose of long-term plans? The primary purpose is to map out the broad tasks for all the branches of the economy. The political leadership may wish to achieve a given rate of growth and a given character of development for a few key sectors. Within this broad outline, it is necessary to fill in many blanks and translate policies into numbers. Once the interconnections are established, the individual tasks may be modified in the light of new directives. As a consequence, even if a plan is changed, the technical work of the planners is not all in vain.

The need for the preparation of relatively detailed long-range plans stems from the absence of a market mechanism which brings the diverse parts of the economy into harmony. Imagine, for instance, that a country decides to expand the airplane industry. In a free-enterprise country, the demand for aluminum, magnesium, and other inputs generated by the expansion of the airplane industry would stimulate supply. In a soviet-type economy, supply does not respond to market demand, since the production of every enterprise is determined by a plan. Thus the expansion of the airplane industry requires a planned expansion of all the cooperating industries or a planned diminution of the use of inputs by other industries. The purpose of the long-term planning process is to establish the interconnection. Should the airplane production plan be modified, the other plans have to be changed accordingly, but the knowledge of the interconnections acquired in the process of long-term planning facilitates the modification of the goals.

b. The Technique of Long-term Planning

The preparation of the plan is a joint enterprise of the political leadership, the administrative and operating units, and the planning body (Gosplan in the Soviet Union, planning commissions in the other countries of the bloc).

On the basis of general political directives, the planning body issues control figures which show the over-all pattern of development during the planned period. The control figures are used as a pattern for the preparation of more detailed plans for the various branches of the economy. This stage requires the cooperation of the economic administrators who have at their disposal better information and more specialized knowledge than is available to the central planning body. In some cases even individual enterprises may be consulted. The detailed programs are returned to the planning body which coordinates them and then introduces modifications necessary to ensure internal consistency. The draft plan is presented for political approval. At this stage—distant from the first steps by a year or more—modifications are often made. These are taken into account in the final plan prepared by the planning body.[20] The final plan, after political approval, becomes law.

[20] For a discussion of the sequence of steps in the preparation of long-range plans in the USSR, see "Les méthodes actuelles soviétiques de planification," *Cahiers de l'institut de science économique appliquée*, Ser. G. no. 7 (August, 1959).

A description of the sequence of administrative steps gives little insight into the planning process itself. It also fails to reveal the nature of the controversy over planning purpose and methodology—a controversy which dates back to the early days of Soviet planning and is still far from being resolved. To show the concrete meaning of the planning process, I shall describe the preparation of the Polish Perspective Plan from 1961 to 1975.

The Polish Perspective Plan for 1961 to 1975 was to provide a framework for three successive plans and to map out the broad sweep of development. The preliminary version of the Perspective Plan served as a foundation for the first draft of the plan for 1959 to 1965. The latter was later amended for political reasons and the Perspective Plan itself never appeared in final form. Nevertheless the Perspective Plan is important for several reasons. It is, without doubt, the most carefully worked out long-range project within the Soviet camp. It also represents what I shall call the "deterministic" tendency in long-term planning.[21]

The over-all task assigned to the planning group (which was headed by Professor Kalecki) was to provide a long-term developmental framework, not only for the fifteen years covered by the plan, but for the period beyond. The

[21] The description of the planning methodology is based on a working paper of the Perspective Plan Institute of the Polish Planning Commission (Komisja Planowania przy Radzie Ministrów, Zakład Planów Perspektywicznych, *Założenia do szczegółowych prac nad planem perspektywicznym na lata 1961–75*, Warszawa, Maj, 1958). I am very grateful to Prof. Bronisław Minc for giving me access to the above document. I have also benefited greatly from interviews with Professor Kalecki and other members of the Institute.

proximate objective was to show by what means Poland could achieve by 1975 the level of consumption currently prevailing in the middle-income Western European countries (such as West Germany) while simultaneously building the foundations for further growth. These objectives were included in a preliminary set of over-all indicators issued in 1957, that is, before the start of detailed investigations.

The over-all objectives made no mention of the time pattern to be followed, but it was implicitly understood that consumption should not be permitted to fall below the initial level at any time covered in the plan.

Seventeen special commissions were entrusted with the elaboration of sections of the plan dealing with individual industries, trade, agriculture, and communications. The commissions included persons of high rank in the economic administration. Other bodies, including regional committees, also took part in the preparation of special reports. The special commissions were asked to base themselves on the over-all indicators, but were issued no detailed instructions. They were also asked to calculate how fast each branch of the economy could grow without running into insurmountable difficulties. At this point it is necessary to mention Professor Kalecki's theory of investment ceilings. According to Professor Kalecki the opportunity cost of development of a branch of industry is fairly constant over a wide range, thus permitting discretionary choice. Beyond a certain rate of development, difficulties mount rapidly. Thus the growth of mining output runs into the barrier created by the long period needed for sinking new shafts; the growth of the chemical industry runs into the barrier caused by the learning period needed to master new processes, etc. By investigating these barriers, Kalecki believes, it is possible to calculate the optimal growth rate, that is, the fastest rate attainable within the raw material and technological constraints.

In addition to determining the optimum rates of growth in their respective branches, the special commissions were asked to analyze the input requirements corresponding to the assumed output levels. Here the current input-output ratios were taken as a basis and were modified in the light of probable technical progress.

The determination of the over-all pattern of growth came at the stage of coordination of the special commissions' reports. Each specialist commission took into account the ceiling relating to its own industry, but not the competing demand on scarce resources. Moreover, there was no coordination in the relative rates of growth. Thus industry A might have planned a higher or lower rate of growth than industries B, C, D, etc., which need A's output as an input. Consequently coordination was needed (1) to ensure that over-all constraints were not violated and (2) to impose internal consistency on the economy.

The constraints within which the Perspective Plan had to fit were first and foremost the availability of labor and of raw materials. Domestic raw materials output was a critical factor. A supply of raw materials from abroad meant an increase in exports and/or a decrease in imports. Given Poland's productive resources and given the probable change in the world's demand, calculations were made to show the maximum amount of foreign currency available. Coal, Poland's traditional major export, faces declining world demand and increasing internal demand (the latter is

a consequence of Poland's industrialization). To substitute
for coal, new exports have to be developed. Rough profitability calculations, combined with projections of probable
world demand, showed that machine tools have to play a
leading export role. The export requirements were incorporated into the production plan. The maximum number of
machine tools (and other commodities) which can be produced domestically, less the number needed for home purposes, determined the probable foreign currency supply.
By this method—through successive approximation—the
foreign raw materials ceiling was determined.

The coordination and analysis of the special commissions' projects yielded an over-all development plan. Using
the projected capital/output ratios for each industry, it was
possible to find global investment requirements. Once the
over-all growth rate was calculated, given the investment
requirements, it was possible to obtain by subtraction the
resources available for consumer goods and services and for
housing.

The results of the calculation show a growth rate of production of material goods equal to 7.1 per cent per annum
and a consumption bill reaching West Germany's 1955 to
1956 level by 1975. These results, according to Kalecki, are
satisfactory. The 7.1 per cent rate of growth is not unrea-
sonable, given the experience of the Soviet Union, West
Germany, Italy, or Japan. A faster rate of growth would
cause excessive tautness in the economy, while with a
slower tempo, it would not be possible to reach the desired
consumption level by 1975.

To determine the final composition of consumption in the

year 1975, Kalecki's team took as a base the consumption pattern of West Germany in the years 1955 and 1956, as well as certain theoretical standards. The program for the food industries, for instance, was based on the physiologists' estimates of what constitutes an excellent diet, as well as on the experience of Germany and the United States. Physiologists claim that advanced countries consume too much sugar and fats. The Perspective Plan wants to keep the consumption of these items at a physiologically optimal level. Since egg production cannot be greatly increased in Poland except by applying more modern methods (which would require substantial investment), egg consumption was projected at 50 per cent of the physiological norm, but the deficiency was to be compensated for by greater consumption of meat. The food plan is thus based on one hand on objective criteria of rational consumption and on the other on scarcity relations.

The plan for clothing lags below the West German standard for 1955 and 1956, because of lack of weaving machinery and balance of trade difficulties. Imports of cotton and wool must be limited because they rank relatively low on the priority list.

The expenditures on alcohol and cigarettes will increase, but their role in the family budget—it is assumed—will be cut by 50 per cent. The cut will occur for "health and social reasons" even though advanced Western countries spend a larger proportion of income on alcohol than Poland. The plan foresees a rapid rise in consumer durables production. By 1975 one out of two households will have a washing machine and one out of every four an electric refrigerator and a vacuum cleaner. The number of passenger automobiles will increase, but because of rubber and fuel supply difficulties will not reach the West European level.

The Perspective Plan for housing is determined by a housing standard which has the following objective: Each family should have a separate apartment, where there must be one separate room for the parents, no more than two children, both of one sex, per room, and a kitchen not used as a bedroom. Construction of cultural and recreational facilities is also often patterned on standards which are theoretically derived from or, more frequently, patterned on Western practice.

Having determined the consumer goods pattern and given the need for further growth beyond 1975, Kalecki's commission established the requirements for the various branches of the capital goods industry. To satisfy export requirements, as well as the requirements of domestic consumer goods production and the requirements of continued growth at a seven per cent rate, there is a need for a certain amount of machine tools. For each machine tool there is need for steel, so that there is a derived demand for steel. The steel-per-machine coefficient was calculated to consider the current tendency toward material saving. Similar calculations were made for the other branches of industry using steel. By iteration the first estimates for machine tools were corrected (machine tool expansion requires steel expansion, but to get more steel, one needs more machine tools) to arrive at a consistent pattern.

The desire to build the foundations for continued expansion beyond the planned period explains the expansion of industries over and above the requirements for 1961 to

1975. Thus steel is needed not only to produce the required output during the period, but also to permit further investment. Paradoxically, the desire to ensure further expansion results in some cases in an output lower than required to satisfy the needs in the planned period. Up to 1975 there will be a great need for housing construction to make up for the backlog. After 1975, the need will be less. If construction facilities were expanded to make up the backlog, some facilities and some construction workers would become superfluous at the end of the plan. Kalecki's team wanted to guard against such an eventuality and decided to limit the size of the construction industry in order to ensure full-capacity operation in the post-1975 period.

The wish to operate all facilities at capacity is characteristic of soviet-type planning. There is a naïve equation between capacity operation and efficiency; idleness suggests loss, while capacity operation suggests good resource use, even though the opposite may be true in some cases. In the plan for 1960 to 1975, no effort was made to compare the loss caused by a delay in housing expansion with the loss of diminishing the size of the industry at some further date. The latter was assumed to be more costly than the former.

The availability of manpower was taken as one of the main limiting factors in Kalecki's plan. The quality of manpower is, however, subject to change. Individual industries reported their needs; on the basis of these needs, a schooling plan was formed. It is clear that manpower needs (like the needs for other inputs) are not absolute; a plant may employ a varying ratio of skilled to unskilled workers and varying amounts of managerial and technical personnel. The technical norms established and used as a basis for the schooling program represent a compromise between the actual state of affairs and the technicians' hopes.

The problem of industrial location was handled by Kalecki's team (as in other long-term plans) as a social as well as an economic question. It was assumed that excessive migration is socially undesirable, and that industry should be brought to the people rather than the reverse, unless there are overwhelming cost considerations to the contrary. The location of industry which is not strongly raw-material oriented is determined by the probable pattern of labor supply.

The sociopolitical approach toward industrial location is a common feature of many soviet-type plans. The location of industry in Soviet Russia is to a large extent determined by social and military factors. In Poland the Six-Year Plan and Kalecki's plan differ in many respects, but location is handled much in the same way in both plans. In his remarks introducing the Six-Year Plan, Hilary Minc (at that time the head of Polish planning) stated that it was important to locate industry so that the predominantly agricultural character of certain areas would be eliminated. Industrial location was also to be used as a means of (1) creating "real bastions of socialism" throughout the country, (2) giving employment to people formerly employed in private trades, and (3) utilizing the available housing space.[22] Kalecki is less explicit in stating what considerations dictate the antimigration policies, but it is clear that there is a desire on one hand to build socialized nuclei throughout the country and on the other to avoid large concentrations of industry and manpower. In practice the location policy is not always consistent, and it vacillates be-

[22] See H. Minc, *op. cit.*, p. 70.

tween industrial dispersion and enlargement of existing centers.

The scheme underlying Kalecki's plan may be summed up as follows. The plan took as a datum the goal of rapid industrial expansion. It also assumed that barriers exist to the rate of expansion. They can be overcome only at an infinite cost. The goal of rapid expansion was quantified and checked against the capacity constraints, in order to obtain an estimate of feasible maximum growth. A calculation was made to see whether the feasible maximum growth will yield a satisfactory consumption pattern. By satisfactory consumption was meant consumption which was rising throughout the plan period and which would reach the West German level of 1955 to 1956 by 1975. The consumption goals had to be modified in view of the most salient scarcity relations. From the given consumption goals and the requirement of growth beyond the planned period, it was possible to calculate the investment needs for the individual producer goods industries.

c. "Determinism" and "Voluntarism" in Long-term Planning

Kalecki's perspective plan as well as the draft plan for the years from 1959 to 1965 met with strong criticism on the part of the policy makers. The plan, the critics said, assumes the inviolability of economic relationships, instead of showing how the relations should be changed through planning. In the words of Eugeniusz Szyr:

The rate of development should be determined by fixing the conditions and goals of socialist industrialization, by the acceleration of growth of the entire economy, and not, as it is

done in the draft of the Seven-Year [1959–65] Plan through an
enumeration of difficulties connected with the rate of growth
of the population, the supply of raw materials, and the construction of housing.[23]

The higher growth rate can be obtained through the elimination of "nonantagonistic contradictions" which, even under socialism, arise "between the economic relations and
the development of productive forces,"[24] that is, through
better organization and harder work.

The revised version of the plan for the first half of the
decade of the 1960s conforms more closely to the prevailing type of the Soviet bloc's long-range plans. The political
leadership dictates specific industrial tasks which become
the cornerstones of the plan. The planners devise ways and
means of fulfilling the tasks. When sufficient resources are
allocated to the key industries and ancillary production necessary to fulfill the set tasks, remaining resources are devoted
to other, less urgent aims. The determination of these sub-
sidiary goals allows for planning flexibility, but the chief
goals are inviolable.

Typically the primary tasks concern basic heavy industries. The output of such industries is treated as an aim in
itself, and it is not derived, as in Kalecki's plan, from the
need for consumer goods; however, in some cases, as in the
current Soviet Seven-Year Plan, certain consumer goods are
specified in the key list.

The approach by which key tasks are politically determined is more voluntaristic than Kalecki's approach in the

[23] Speech of E. Szyr at the 12th Plenum of the Central Committee of the PZPR, Warsaw, 1958 (mimeographed).
[24] *Ibid.*

sense that the former puts prime emphasis on the willful transformation of the economy, and the latter on the determination of the underlying functional relationships. The demarcation lines between the two approaches are now rather blurred, but at one time they were very sharply drawn.

During the Soviet industrialization debate of the 1920s,[25] the deterministic school insisted on the necessity of performing economic calculations in the formation of plans and also on the essential inviolability of underlying economic relations. The extreme wing of this faction looked upon planning as a method of long-range projection, that is, as a forecast of future development rather than as a tool for development.

Stripped of the heavy ideological and polemical overlay, the extreme deterministic view is that planning should be determined by the efficiency of investment as measured by the satisfaction of material wants of the population. Under deterministic planning the nation's resources and the population's needs dictate the rate and character of economic evolution. Carried to its logical conclusion the deterministic view asks planners to play a quasi-market game, as in the Lange system.

The voluntaristic faction looked upon planning as a tool for transforming the economy in accordance with the will of the policy makers. The economic relations prevailing in a country at the time of the socialist take-over reflect the capitalist mode of organization. Socialism can rebuild the

[25] See A. Erlich, "Preobrajensky and the Economics of Soviet Industrialization," *Quarterly Journal of Economics*, vol. 64, no. 1, February, 1950.

economy from its foundations. In doing so, the leadership should not look at the present state of affairs, but should be guided by the picture of the future socialist state. In the reconstruction of the economy, current needs should not be taken as a supreme consideration, since the socialist state is made not only for the present, but also for the generations to come.

One of the main points of contention in the industrialization debate was the relative rate of development of industry and agriculture. The deterministic faction pointed out the need for "balance" between the two sectors of the economy, while the voluntaristic wing insisted on the desirability of rapid industrialization. The development of industry in the latter view is essential to lay the foundations of a future prosperous society and also to ensure the growth of the proletariat, the backbone of the socialist state. It is interesting to note that although an understanding of the issues at stake has deepened since the 1920s and although the standpoints of both factions have changed, the agriculture versus industry issue is reopened whenever the need for economic calculations is debated.

The voluntaristic approach triumphed with the consolidation of Stalin's power in the Soviet Union, and it was maintained through the 1940s. Plans in that period concentrated almost exclusively on the execution of the key tasks set by the political leadership. In these key areas, latest available production techniques were applied with little regard to over-all scarcity relations. Leftover resources were apportioned to the remaining sectors of the economy. The low priority sectors also had planned goals, but these were readily sacrificed when the fulfillment of key tasks demanded it.

Voluntaristic planning resulted in rapid growth of key sectors, especially of heavy industry and armaments, but it also imposed great hardships on the population. Since little thought and effort were spared for the determination of rational resource use, resources were being wasted at a staggering rate. The mistakes ultimately led Stalin to a guarded retreat from the voluntaristic stand. In 1952, Stalin declared that laws of economic development are objective. They must be conformed to and cannot be changed at will by the political leadership.[26] This statement permitted the reopening of a debate on rational criteria for planning.

After Stalin's death, the debate on rationality in planning became more open and vigorous. Much of the debate concerned the choice of investment criteria for individual projects, an issue which will be discussed briefly in connection with short-term planning. The question of over-all planning goals was also reopened, rather timidly in the Soviet Union, and in a much more outspoken fashion in Poland.

In the post-Stalin debate it became clear that two vastly distinct issues were at stake. The first issue is: Who should set the goals of long-range development; the second: How to ensure the efficient fulfillment of the goals, no matter how and why they are set.

The goal-setting debate was prejudged from the first. Though in Poland there was some revival of interest in the Lange scheme of quasi-market planning, there was never a possibility that the political leadership would abandon its economic power and let the wishes of the consumers dictate the development of the economy. Since Stalin's death, ef-

[26] J. Stalin, *Economic Problems of Socialism in the USSR,* New York, International Publishers, 1952. Quotation from the Polish edition (Warszawa, Książka l Wiedza), 1952, p. 92.

forts have been made to ascertain consumers' wishes and follow them whenever possible, but decision making firmly rests with the political authorities. In fact, Kalecki's plans (which do not even propose to restore consumer sovereignty in any way) paid too much attention to the wishes of consumers to be acceptable.

The debate concerning goal-fulfillment methods is of more interest, and it is quite likely that ultimately it will result in a profound transformation of the soviet-type planning system. The reform proposals concentrate on efficient resource use in conformity with the goals set by the Party leaders.

The most sweeping proposal would ask the planning office to prepare a vast array of alternative plans, showing the efficient resource use given alternative goals. The political authorities would then choose the program which suits them best.[27] Such an approach seems theoretically possible, but the practical difficulties are insurmountable. The preparation of a grand transformation function for the whole economy requires the knowledge of factor and product substitution possibilities throughout the economy, not only at a point of time, but for the duration of the proposed plan. For the present and the foreseeable future, there is no possibility of obtaining the relevant information and making the necessary calculations.

Critical attention focuses on proposals made in the Soviet Union by Kantorovich, a mathematician who can claim priority in the development of linear programming. Kantoro-

[27] For an English summary and discussion of the view of Kantorovich, see Benjamin Ward, "Kantorovich on Economic Calculation," *Journal of Political Economy*, vol. 68, no. 6, 1960.

vich leaves the goal-setting task to the leadership. Once the desired output quantities are determined, the allocation of resources to fulfill or overfulfill the goals is to be determined by mathematical programming. The task is confined to input allocation given one output mix, yet its magnitude is staggering.

Kantorovich's proposal to program the economy is at once threatening to the leadership and insufficient for long-term planning purposes. The threat lies in the calculation of "shadow prices" which reveal the implicit cost of the leadership's program. The use of computational methods also cuts down the discretionary powers of the leadership to the making of over-all decisions. These considerations— as well as the formidable practical difficulties—are likely (at least for the present) to relegate programming to the solution of individual problems, to the exclusion of grand over-all calculations.

For the present, practical efforts at improving resource allocation efficiency are confined to the elimination of visible waste and better coordination of product flows within the economy. The lack of such coordination and poor timing of investment projects during the 1930s and 1940s accounted for numerous bottlenecks and surpluses, which threatened to defeat the leadership's basic purposes:

> The negative results of economic disproportions manifest themselves in the form of disturbances in the over-all economic development of the nation and in the lowering of the efficiency of investment. In the final count economic disproportions slow down the progress of the Socialist transformation of society.[28]

[28] Gomułka's speech at the 3d Congress of the PZPR, see *III zjazd PZPR*, Warszawa, Książka i Wiedza, 1959, p. 81.

The coordination of long-range development programs consists of matching proposed outputs with proposed uses. This type of coordination, known as material balancing, has been a central feature of soviet-type long-range planning ever since the first Soviet Five-Year Plan, yet until recently the results were very defective. Balancing over a number of years in a rapidly changing economy necessarily involves much guesswork, and long experience is necessary before reasonable results can be achieved. Moreover, as long as a radical form of voluntarism ruled supreme, the process of balancing was not permitted to interfere with decision making. As a consequence, planners had to strike balances which represented the leadership's hopes and wishes without much regard to the underlying technological conditions. In recent years, however, balancing has received great emphasis, since it is felt that lack of coordination, rather than coordination, is a threat to the leadership.

Balancing is a method of securing the consistency of a plan, and strictly speaking, it is not a method of optimizing. Yet within the context of a soviet-type economy, balancing is a step toward better use of resources. Once the development goals have been chosen and the selection of techniques has been made, the better the balancing and the greater the output out of given inputs. Thus better balancing of soviet-type economies is a step toward improved resource allocation.[29] It is also a step which is acceptable to the advocates of deterministic planning and to all but the most intransigent voluntarists.

[29] Włodzimierz Brus, *Ogólne problemy funkcjonowania gospodarki socjalistycznej*, Warszawa, Państwowy Instytut Wydawniczy, 1961, p. 118.

d. The Selection of Development Goals

While the right of the leadership to set development goals is never seriously questioned by the supporters of the soviet-type system, the proper method of goal selection remains an important issue. None of the current proposals to improve allocative efficiency gives the leadership any guidance in this respect. Yet the leadership must translate into concrete tasks its basic desire to achieve fast growth of output and to build up heavy industry. The planners who interpret and quantify the leadership's desires (and who thereby have a strong influence on the nature of long-range plans) must also have a general guideline.

The simplest method of long-term planning is to subdivide the economy into sectors of special interest to the political leadership and to assume that within a given sector the output of all products must grow at the same rate. The leadership determines the growth of relevant key outputs, such as the armament industries, the investment goods industries, etc., while the detailed plans are prepared by simple extrapolation. This method is widely criticized as being based on a "vulgar error" in reasoning, yet it still wields considerable influence in the practice of long-range planning.[30]

A somewhat more sophisticated approach takes as its starting point the experience of more advanced nations, especially the free-enterprise countries.[31] Such a method is most readily understandable in the planning of consumer

[30] M. Rakowski, *op. cit.*, pp. 28ff.
[31] *Ibid.*, p. 112.

goods production, and indeed, it is widely practiced as a forecasting device in free-enterprise nations.

In drawing up the consumer goods plans, planners strive to satisfy the needs of the consumers, as long as such needs do not conflict with the other goals of the leadership. The plan maps out investments which will satisfy the population's future needs. By the time the goods are produced, incomes will be higher than they are at the planning stage. To satisfy consumer needs, it is important to ascertain what such needs will be at the higher income level. Comparisons with the actual purchase pattern in more advanced countries give a convenient starting point for the preparation of the plans.

The observed pattern of wants is not binding to the policy makers. Consumers are ill-informed, they are subject to outside influences, and they do not always know what is good for them. Moreover, even in a soviet-type system, they are selfish and make choices without regard to the over-all national goals:

> National ownership, in its present form, means that each individual is only indirectly an owner of the means of production. As a consequence people put the satisfaction of their individual wants in the first place.[32]

The Party, as repository of national interest, has the duty of influencing the consumption pattern and correcting consumers' choice whenever objective criteria (such as dietary standards) are available.

In drawing up consumer goods plans, foreign prototypes

[32] Ber Haus and Przemysław Kotlarek, "Cel gospodarki socjalistycznej a cel przedsiębiorstwa," *Gospodarka Planowa*, vol. 15, no. 12, p. 26, 1960.

are not followed slavishly, because the plans reflect local scarcity relations. The heavy priority assigned to the development of basic industries has kept back the output of metal-using consumer durables as compared with the consumption patterns of free-enterprise countries. Were the consumers free to choose, they might well elect to have less to eat and drive more cars, but their desires are never put to a test. The production objectives are set by the leadership, not by the consumers; the leadership is willing to guess at the consumers' wishes, but not to let the consumers influence the choice.

The utilization of foreign experience in the planning of producer goods industries is at first less understandable than the patterning of consumer goods assortment after the free-market countries. Producer goods industry structure under free enterprise reflects the demand for consumer goods. In the soviet-type economies, producer goods are largely planned for future growth. Yet, even in the soviet-type economies, the distant goal is consumer goods output. The build-up of heavy industry is an aim in itself as far as the present is concerned, but in the future, industrial might will be used to satisfy the population's needs. Thus the structure achieved by the advanced free-enterprise countries serves as a useful bench-mark for development planning.

It is clear that two of the basic programs of soviet-type planning—electrification and the development of steel industry—are patterned after the capitalist nations, especially the United States. Electrification was one of the principal goals anteceding even the Five-Year Plans, and it still is kept at the forefront. Thus Poland's current plan sets a high goal for electrification because "the statistics of industrial development of Western Europe, the United States, Czechoslovakia, and the Soviet Union show systematically that the output of industrial energy expands faster than industrial output as a whole." [33] Even the emphasis on the development of the iron and steel industry can be traced to comparisons with free-enterprise nations. Throughout the world there is a naïve tendency to use the steel output as an index of economic achievement. By concentrating on steel, Soviet-bloc countries symbolically "catch up" with the advanced free-enterprise nations.

Despite the use of free-enterprise models in the preparation of long-term plans, the development of Soviet-bloc countries differs radically from that of free-enterprise nations. Investments in free-enterprise countries are made in response to expected profitability, that is, in response to needs which become manifest within the economy. Investments in the soviet-type economies are made to transform the economy and achieve a desired pattern. In one case growth is organic; it is the result of many individual decisions. In another, growth follows a predetermined path, and investment decisions are subordinate to the over-all pattern.

e. Summary and Conclusions

Planners in the Soviet-bloc countries express in long-range plans the political leadership's program to transform and develop the economy of the nation. Politically, the plans serve to gather support for a common set of goals and to show the results which the common effort is expected to yield. Technically, the plans are a check on the

[33] E. Szyr, *op. cit.*, p. 36.

feasibility of policies and a framework for detailed directives.

Long-term plans have no operational significance, and the operational plans and directives often deviate from the course initially mapped out. Nevertheless, multiperiod plans are of great importance, for they show how the various sectors of the economy depend on each other. The interrelations thus discovered are utilized even if the course of action has to be changed.

All long-term plans aim to transform the economy, though some come close to deterministic forecasts, while others look at the economy as a completely pliable body. The former type of plan allocates resources in accordance with their availability and the needs of the population. The latter tends to neglect needs and resources and to be guided purely by a vision of the future.

To make a long-term plan it is necessary to choose development goals. As a general rule the Soviet-bloc countries seek to reach the level of advanced capitalist nations and take the advanced countries' product mix as a goal. That goal is to be reached through planning, not through the organic growth process of free-enterprise nations. The plans indicate the means by which the desired production levels are to be reached.

Long-term plans give an over-all sketch of the edifice, but to construct the building it is necessary to have detailed blueprints and directives. To understand how the construction is made and how the elements are chosen and fitted together, we must turn to short-term economic and institutional plans which are the working documents in the soviet-type system.

5

Short-term Planning

The broad pattern of development of soviet-type economies is mapped out in statements of policy makers and in perspective and long-range plans. All such documents are declarations of intent; they state what should be done, but do not indicate how policies are to be put into action. The task of translating objectives into directives is left to the short-term planners.

The purpose of short-term plans is to determine "the most effective use of available resources in accordance with the [goal outlined in] five-year plans." [1] To draft a short-term plan, it is necessary to have detailed, up-to-date information on the productive capacity of the economy. The tasks given to the economy must be consistent with productive capac-

[1] Polish Planning Commission, *Economic Planning in Poland: Remarks on Aims and Methods* (mimeographed, n.d.), p. 10. This document was prepared by the Polish Planning Commission for the United Nations.

ity; hence, a careful check must be made of the consistency and feasibility of the economic program. The check involves considerations of alternate use of available resources and alternate production goals.

Short-term plans have a directive force, and the plans must be translated into action. In looking at the method of enforcement of a plan, we are leaving economic for institutional planning. At the directive level the connection between the two kinds of plans is extremely close. For example, a short-term plan which specifies in minute detail the productive tasks of individual enterprises requires the transmittal of a large number of directives from the top administrative level to the operating level. On the other hand, a plan which indicates only the broad aggregates of products makes an implicit assumption that product-mix decisions are made at some other level. Typically (though not inevitably), detailed planning is associated with an institutional system which relies on directives, while aggregate planning leans more toward decentralization of decision making and reliance on indirect incentives.

Short-term planning does not require the broad vision needed in the preparation of long-term plans. Instead, short-term planners must deal with allocation details and be concerned with the system of economic administration. The task of investigating short-term plans might not seem very glamorous. Yet if we want to understand how the soviet-type economy actually functions, we must look at the short-term plans.

Soviet-type planning rests on the foundation of physical allocation, and short-term plans are no exception to this rule. The plan is an enumeration of goods and services to be produced. Prices are used merely as physical aggregation weights held constant over long periods to facilitate comparisons among different plans. The fixed (comparable) prices play no allocative role, and they have no operational meaning other than that of aggregation.

While planning is carried out in physical terms, economic transactions in the soviet-type economies are carried out in terms of money values. The linkage between physical allocation and financial transactions is provided by the financial plans which restate the economic program in terms of prices at which the transactions are carried out.[2]

Financial planning is necessary to coordinate the money-wage payments with the prices set on consumer goods. Wages allocate labor to jobs, and consumer goods prices allocate the available goods to the wage earners; the two markets must be linked in the plan. Financial planning also facilitates coordination of the sectors of the economy under different types of control. Directly owned state enterprises deal on a commercial basis with cooperatives, enterprises under regional control, and privately owned enterprises. Within the sector of direct national ownership, the financial accounts are of less importance, since all transfers are internal to the vast state enterprise. Yet even within the state sector, financial planning is useful. Each enterprise is a separate accounting unit, and financial planning eases the task of coordination and performance control. Finally, financial planning serves as a control device over the co-operative and private sectors. These sectors do not work in accordance with a physical plan, and the allocation of

---

[2] Since the long-term and perspective plans have no directive significance, there are no financial long-term plans.

their product to consumption and investment is accomplished through price, taxation, and credit policies specified in the financial plan.

Physical as well as financial short-term plans aim at an efficient resource allocation. Long-range plans lay out the broad lines of development, but details of resource use are decided for the most part on a short-term basis. The calculations do not appear explicitly in the plans, but they constitute an integral part of the preparatory work.

Although the line between short-term planning and the implementation of short-term plans is difficult to draw, I shall endeavor to consider the two questions separately. This chapter will be concerned primarily with the preparation of the plans.[3] How the plans are put into practice will be the main subject of Chapter 6.

a. Preparation of the Draft Plan

Short-term physical plans are the joint product of the Planning Commission, the economic ministries, and the operating units within the economy. The process of short-term planning is continuous. A plan comes into effect at the beginning of the year, at which time the results of the performance of the previous plan are being evaluated. Almost immediately work starts on the plan for the succeed-

[3] An excellent description of the short-term planning process in the Soviet Union is given by Herbert Levine, "The Centralized Planning of Supply in the Soviet Union," in Joint Economic Committee, Congress of the United States, *Comparisons of the United States and Soviet Economies*, United States Government Printing Office, 1960, pp. 154–175. Except for some minor details, this process is identical in all the Soviet-bloc countries.

ing year. That plan is elaborated and improved throughout the year, and changes are made in the light of actual performance. Simultaneously, the performance of the plan for the current year must be controlled and additional orders issued if necessary.

Early in spring (March or April) the Central Planning Office issues a set of "preliminary indicators" (called "control figures" in the Soviet Union), as the first draft plan for the succeeding year is called. The indicators are closer in character to a forecast than to a plan. The figures for 1962, for instance, are based on the actual performance in 1960 and on a preliminary appraisal of probable results in 1961. Before the final plan is completed, the over-all situation may undergo substantial changes.

The indicators, prepared with the cooperation of the economic ministries and in consultation with the political authorities, sketch out the broad outline of the program for the planned year. The outline shows employment, income generation, income distribution, and investment. It indicates the production of commodities by product groups and gives detailed schedules for major commodities. The magnitude of the most important investment projects is also indicated.

In drafting the indicators, the Planning Commission bases itself on the long-range plans without following them slavishly. Actual performance of the economy must be taken into account, and so must changes in the policy makers' desires. In general, in the later years of a long-range plan, the discrepancies between the original project and actual developments are considerable.

The indicators have a twofold function: They provide a

framework for the drafting of detailed projects by the economic administrators, and they serve as a request for information to be transmitted to the Central Planning Commission.

Each set of indicators is accompanied by detailed instructions showing how to draft the plans for enterprises
and branches of industry. As the indicators are transferred
to the lower levels of economic administration, they are
elaborated in more detail. Enterprise plans are drafted at
the working level. These are transmitted upward, aggre-
gated, and finally presented to the Commission. The Commission thus receives not only detailed projects drafted in
accordance with a uniform pattern, but also up-to-date information on the performance of the economy.

In drafting their projects the enterprises are asked to
show what physical and financial resources they will need
to achieve the planned levels of output. The estimates of inputs must conform to technical and financial norms imposed
by the Planning Commission and the economic ministries.
The norms specify the maximum inputs permissible per
unit output. The major operations are described in terms
of technical norms, specifying the man-hours per unit of
output, the use of raw materials, semifabricates, and power.
Complex operations are regulated by so-called "statistical
norms," based on aggregate input-output relations observed in the past. The norms are altered over time in response to technological progress.

Financial norms deal with aggregates rather than with
individual processes. Based on the expected physical performance and a schedule of prices, each enterprise must
show the expected aggregate wage payments, the purchases

of products from other enterprises, the value of expected inventory holdings, etc. The financial project will ultimately be used in the determination of the amount of available finance, and the physical project will be used in real resource allocation.

At the time of the preparation of the draft enterprise projects, details of the output mix are yet to be settled; hence, the drafts must be couched in general terms. The machine-tool industry, for instance, may indicate the over-all volume of production and the over-all input requirements. The preparation of a detailed output program must await the exact determination of needs for various kinds of machines. Since the input needs of the machine tool industry depend on the nature of the output mix, precise input requirements also can only be determined at a later time.

If enterprises are not able to carry out their tasks within existing capacity, they must outline plans for expansion. These plans must also conform to technical and financial norms. In choosing a given type of investment, the enterprise must perform calculations showing the technical superiority of the choice over alternate solutions. These calculations must conform to detailed instructions issued by the Planning Commission.

Major investment projects transgress the framework of a given enterprise and a single annual plan. Whenever need arises for the establishment of a separate productive unit, studies are made at the respective ministry in cooperation with the Planning Commission. The indicators take the major projects into account, although the final decision comes in all cases at the time of the acceptance of the finished plan.

The performance information furnished by the enterprises and the draft enterprise plans are utilized by the
Planning Commission for the preparation of a draft national plan. The conceptual difficulties of drafting the plan
are considerable. The indicators which served as a basis
for the enterprise plans were based on outdated information, and they dealt with broad aggregates rather than
with details. The enterprise plans were based on the indicators; hence, the use of the enterprise plans to correct the
indicators feeds back the original bias. On the other hand,
the enterprise plans cannot simply be updated in the light
of the newly received performance information. The difficulty encountered here may best be explained on the basis
of an example.

Imagine that the indicators prescribe a 10 per cent increase in output of a product for 1963 as compared with
the planned level for 1962. Enterprises make their plans
in accordance with the indicator, but at the same time they
show that the plan for 1962 will be over-fulfilled by 10 per
cent. In the light of this new information, the basis of the
plan for 1963 has to be shifted, yet a simple extrapolation
may run into capacity barriers requiring further expansion.
The enterprise projects based on the indicators do not show
the additional inputs needed if expansion is to be undertaken. To get an accurate picture, it would be necessary to
issue a revised set of indicators and to obtain a new set of
preliminary enterprise projects.

Difficulties also arise from the uncertainty concerning
the relationship between the preliminary indicators and
the enterprise plans. The indicators are supposed to be
guideposts, not blueprints. If they are considered blue-

prints, then the Planning Commission receives back the same information which it sent out in the first place. If they are guideposts, the question becomes how and why enterprises introduced the changes. In general, it is in the interest of enterprises to have easy, planned tasks; hence, enterprises tend to lower the output goals outlined in the indicators and to increase the input requirements. To justify the changes, enterprises also present a pessimistic picture of the current year's plan fulfillment. As a consequence, the planning process assumes the character of a bilateral bargain instead of being a cooperative effort. This aspect of planning will occupy us further in the next chapter.

In the absence of objective and reliable information, the preparation of a draft national plan is more an art than a science. From long practice, planners know that the pessimistic picture given in the enterprise reports will change by the end of the planning year. At that time, performance premiums are calculated, and plans which seemed impossible to accomplish are reported as overfulfilled. Thus the proper base for the next plan must be estimated from relations observed in the past between preliminary and final performance reports. Even there, a simple extrapolation cannot be made since the inducements to underestimate past production or overestimate input requirements change over time in response to changes in the institutional plan. The planners must take all the changes into account and arrive at an over-all estimate of the bias.

The preparation of a draft plan would be infinitely difficult were it not for the routine character of planning. For most of the products each annual plan is much like its predecessor, except for a growth factor. Specialists dealing

year after year with the same branch of industry develop
a "feeling" for a properly drawn plan, and they can readily
spot inconsistencies and exaggerations.

Since draft-plan figures are not publicly available, the
hypothesis of the routine character of planning may only
be tested on the final plan figures. Let us perform the
test before returning to the problem of the preparation of
the plan.

If the hypothesis that short-term planning is mostly simple extrapolation is true, then it should be possible to explain actual production levels by extrapolating the past
trend. The statistical data published by the Polish Central
Statistical Office permits a modest test of the hypothesis.
Planned outputs and output fulfillments are given for 1959.
The list for 1958 is not strictly comparable, but of the 77
products in the 1959 list, 57 established products also
appear in the 1958 list.[4] The correlation of the percentage
output increases planned for 1959 with the actual output
increase yields a coefficient of .96. The correlation of the
percentage output increases achieved in 1958 with the percentage output increases achieved in 1959 yields a coefficient of .94. The difference between the two coefficients

[4] Główny Urząd Statystyczny, *Biuletyn Statystyczny,* no. 1,
1959, and no. 2, 1960. The classification of products into old
and new is somewhat arbitrary. Some of the new products were
not included in the 1958 list, while in the case of others planned
production increases amounted to 250 per cent or more. For
the established products, planned increases did not surpass 35
per cent. The inclusion of the new products lowers the correlation between 1958 increases and 1959 increases to an insignificant level.

is insignificant, hence the test lends support to the extrapolation hypothesis.

Where new products are introduced, the extrapolation technique is replaced by a technique of forecasting: Given the available facilities and the scheduled completion of new investment objectives, the probable output of the new product is forecast. The forecast is included in the plan and it achieves the objective status of a directive.

Realistic and feasible plans for individual branches of industry do not constitute a feasible over-all plan. All the plans in the aggregate may put excessive pressure on the use of certain resources, such as labor. Moreover, the output plans of an industry may not be identical with the planned needs of industries using that output as a productive factor. Branch plans must be "balanced" to yield a consistent and feasible national plan. This process is accomplished in the soviet-type economies by the process of "material balances."

b. The Process of "Material Balancing"

To explain the nature of material balancing, let us imagine that planning is carried out in a stationary economy. The planners have a complete record of the previous year's inputs and outputs and interindustry flows. If in the previous year there was no accumulation or decumulation anywhere in the economy, the plan is a replica of the previous year's pattern. Likewise, if all parts of the economy grow at a constant proportional rate, the plan is a scaled-up version of the previous plan. In neither case is there any necessity for complex balancing to ensure the consistency of a plan.

Imagine now that the previous year's plan was improperly drawn, so that shortages developed in some sectors and surpluses in others. A repetition of the previous year's pattern would produce the same unwanted results. A partial approach will provide only partial relief. Imagine, for instance, that there is a shortage of steel in the munitions industry. To remedy the shortage, steel is channeled away from less essential industries, such as construction. If construction can be carried out with less steel, the problem is solved, albeit not necessarily in a most efficient fashion. As a matter of practical policy, such *ad hoc* directives are frequently resorted to if a plan turns out to be badly balanced. Instead of recalculating all relations, directives deflect the use of critical materials to their most essential uses. Less essential branches must find substitutes or their production comes to a stop.

If allocation by *ad hoc* directive is to be avoided, the next year's plan must make provision for greater production of steel and/or lesser use of steel. Such changes require a thorough rebalancing of the whole economy. If, for instance, steel is to expand at a faster rate than it has so far, so must the production of the factors used by the steel industry. If these factors in turn utilize steel, a secondary correction must be made in the steel program. Thus, every change in the goals of production and every correction of past mistakes requires a rebalancing of the whole system.

Soviet practice relies on a flexible and informal system of balancing which shuns a strict mathematical formulation. The process starts with a summing up of the input requirements for each product by all the producers. The requirements are then compared with the supply, calculated by reviewing all the planned outputs. Major factors of production are treated individually, while aggregate balances are prepared for miscellaneous products of lesser importance.

When the supply side of a balance fails to equal the demand side, adjustments are necessary. In the case of some factors, such as labor, the supply is fixed and adjustment must take place on the demand side. The adjustment can take the form either of coefficient modification or production curtailment. For instance, the transport industry's demand for workers can be curtailed either by requiring the industry to provide the planned transport with fewer workers or by curtailing the transport plans. Which course will be adopted depends on the substitution possibilities, or to be more precise, on the knowledge of substitution possibilities.

In deciding what to trim and how to trim, consultations with the economic administrators and the policy makers play an important role. The administrators have a better idea of the economy's existing slack spots where trimming could be done without much injury. When a cutback in output is inevitable, the approval of the policy makers is essential.

Adjustments in balance in soviet-type economies are made by a method of successive approximation. Effects of the adjustment of one balance are traced to other balances, and each balance is adjusted in turn. The method is time consuming, and the solution is not exact. Attempts to expedite and improve the balancing process have led in recent years to a search for a more "scientific" approach, and numer-

ous suggestions were made both within and outside the
Soviet sphere that the Leontief scheme should replace material balancing. Experimental matrices for the whole
economy have been drawn in accordance with the Leontief
scheme in the Soviet Union, Poland, Hungary, and other
countries engaging in soviet-type planning, though there is
no indication that they are to supersede material balancing.

The Leontief scheme [5] represents the economy in the
form of a set of linear equations. Each equation shows the
total output of a sector of the economy and the utilization
of that output by all the sectors. For instance, one equation shows how the total output of steel is divided among
the various users, such as the coal mining industry, the
construction industry, the transport industries, and the other
steel-using sectors.

In addition to showing the distribution of each type of
output among the users, the Leontief system shows the
relations between inputs and outputs. For instance, a
given amount of coal, iron ore, scrap, and other inputs is
consumed in the production of steel. The input-output
relationships cannot be expressed in the form of a simple
summation, since the diverse inputs are qualitatively different. To overcome this difficulty, Leontief expresses inputs as well as outputs in value terms. Each input-output
equation states that the total value of output is equal to the
sum of the values of inputs, including human labor.

[5] For a simple explanation of the Leontief model and solution
methods, see W. D. Evans and M. Hoffenberg, "The Inter-
industry Relations Study for 1947," *Review of Economics and
Statistics*, vol. 34, May, 1952. See also Robert W. Campbell,
Soviet Economic Power, Boston, Houghton Mifflin Company,
1960, chap. 5.

With a given technology it is possible to calculate how much of each type of input is needed to produce one unit of a given type of output. Once this technological datum is obtained, it is readily possible to build up a consistent inter-industry flow pattern for any set of final demands.

To demonstrate the use of the input-output technique, assume once again that the planners wish to increase the net output of steel over a base period. The desired increase is stated as a final demand. By inverting an input-output matrix the planners will immediately see how much coal and iron, transport and labor, and other goods and services will be needed to obtain more steel. Some of these goods and services are needed directly to produce more steel, while others are needed to produce goods which in turn are used in steel production. The calculation will also show how much steel expansion will be needed to sustain the level of additional production of the various goods needed for steel making. The solution is rapid and exact.

The problem of finding a consistent flow pattern yielding a desired set of final products can be solved by material balancing, but the solution is exceedingly laborious. To solve the increase in steel output problems, the following steps are necessary. First it is important to find out how much more input will be directly needed by the steel industry in order to increase output by the desired amount. Let there be need, say, for x more coal, y more iron, and z more transport units. Now the balances for coal, iron, and transport have to be adjusted. To produce more coal, iron, and transport, one must increase the quantities of other inputs. If one of these inputs is steel, the steel balance must be rebalanced in order to take into account the secondary demand. This adjustment starts a second round of approximations, and a readjustment of the iron, coal, and transport balance. The process continues until the desired degree of accuracy is achieved.

While by a process of successive approximations it is possible to approximate a Leontief solution, the fact that all the balances are "balanced" does not indicate the solution has been reached. Unlike the Leontief system, the system of material balances does not show the magnitude of technical coefficients. Thus it is possible to balance each commodity and achieve an over-all balance by violating the technical capacity of the economy. In reality such pseudo-balancing occurs rather frequently because the matching of inputs from one balance with the outputs from another presents great difficulties. The diverse balances differ in the degree of aggregation, and often there are differences in definitions of various commodities. Indeed much effort is currently expended in the Soviet Union as well as in Poland to standardize the balances—a prerequisite to a genuine iterative solution.

Despite its obvious advantages, the Leontief system is not wholly acceptable to soviet-type planners. Leaving aside considerations of Marxist ideology, it is a problem whether the assumptions underlying the Leontief system can be accepted for purposes of planning. These assumptions are of fundamental importance, and they are responsible for the ease with which a mathematical solution can be obtained.

The Leontief system makes two fundamental postulates: (1) labor is the only scarce factor and (2) the input-output coefficients are fixed. Neither of these assumptions is useful for short-term planning.

One of the fundamental problems of short-term planning is how to utilize existing capacity. In making balancing adjustments, planners must reckon with capacity limitations which limit the possibility of upward adjustments in balances. Moreover, the labor scarcity assumption is quite inappropriate for several of the countries in the Soviet orbit which have a fast-growing labor force and often underutilize their manpower. When labor shortages occur, they take the form of excess demand for a specific skill, rather than an over-all demand for manpower.

Capacity limitations can be taken into account in the course of balancing, since each balance is treated as a separate entity. In a Leontief system, where the solution is carried simultaneously for the whole economy, capacity limitations cannot be included so easily. True, it is possible to partition the Leontief matrix and obtain solutions for subsectors, thus making sure that capacity limits are not violated. The abandonment of the over-all approach is tantamount to the abandonment of simplicity, and the superiority of the Leontief solution becomes more questionable.

In preparing material balances, planning technicians search for possibilities of increasing outputs without a proportional increase in all inputs. Thus, the successive approximation method permits balancing through coefficient modification. In the Leontief system, too, coefficients can be modified, but only at a cost of considerable complication in the solution method. In the final count when the Leontief approach is modified to a sufficient extent to be of use in short-term balancing, its greatest virtue—solution simplicity—is largely lost.

The contrast between the flexibility of material balancing and the inflexibility of input-output is understood by planners in the soviet-type economies:

The main advantage of the approach used in practice [i.e., of material balancing] is that we are not obliged to make any aprioristic assumptions about functional (in fact proportional) relationships between variables. We can (in theory, at any rate) take into account in every step of sectoral analysis different relationships between changes in variables.[6]

Thus, whereas the input-output system assumes the existence of constant factor proportions, planners with material balances can alter (within limits) the factor proportions prevailing in the economy.

Despite the difficulties and limitations in the use of the Leontief scheme for short-term planning, mathematical methods are gaining increasing acceptance as old-fashioned bureaucrats are replaced by mathematically trained technicians. Mathematical programming finds use in the solution of problems involving capacity limitations, while broad input-output calculations are made to ensure over-all consistency of plans. As yet these methods do not yield striking results because of inherent limitations in the data. Performance reports are inaccurate, and they come in with a considerable time lag. Worst of all, the statement of policy goals cannot readily be quantified, and the goals themselves are subject to modification in the course of the balancing process.

The level at which a commodity is "balanced" and the method of its allocation depend on the importance of the

[6] Polish Planning Commission, *Economic Planning in Poland*, p. 23.

commodity to the national economy and also on the conditions of supply. Inputs which are of major importance to several branches of the economy and which are in short supply are individually balanced by the Central Planning Commission. Quotas of the "deficit" or "funded" commodities are allocated to individual enterprises. Enterprises which receive insufficient quotas are forced to substitute inputs which are not on the funded list.

The list of deficit or funded commodities tended to be extremely long during the Stalinist regime and often included several thousand positions. In the post-Stalin reforms the list was radically curtailed in all Soviet-bloc countries. In Poland it underwent a most radical pruning and now comprises only a few score items.

Products which are not on the funded or deficit list are balanced on the Planning Commission level in terms of aggregates. Many such products are balanced in detail by the ministry which is chiefly concerned. For instance, the ministry of heavy industry compiles balances of all machine tools and designates machine-tool quotas for the individual factories. Finally, there are less important products for which balances are struck after the enterprise orders come in, much in the way free-enterprise suppliers adjust their product mix to the customers' demand. The recent trend puts emphasis on flexibility; the list of articles balanced on the basis of enterprise orders is growing. Thus while in 1956, 79.6 per cent of assortments were centrally planned, by 1959 the percentage declined to 55.4 per cent—the rest being balanced on the basis of enterprise orders.[7]

[7] Rada Ekonomiczna przy Radzie Ministrów, *Sytuacja ekonomiczna kraju w roku 1959*, p. 41.

The balancing process completes the preparation of the draft plan, and heralds the last phase of the planning process, the construction of the final version of the plan, which has a binding force on the economy.

c. Completion of the Short-term Physical Plan

The draft plan presented by the Planning Commission to the political authorities is based on more recent information than the indicators. It is also carefully balanced and contains all the items which will enter the final plan. Yet the draft is often less acceptable politically than the preliminary indicators. The indicators reflected the leadership's aims as of early spring, while the draft plan is completed in the late fall. In the intervening months new economic facts come to light, and the leadership may also change some of its goals. Moreover, the draft plan rarely follows the indicators very closely, and the modifications may be little to the liking of the government.

The changes required by the policy makers necessitate a rebalancing of the plan, for which there usually is no time. In practice the adjustments are made in a makeshift fashion, and the final plan is usually less carefully balanced than the draft. If the political modifications are substantial, the final plan may also be less realistic than the earlier version.

After final approval by political authorities, the national plan acquires a directive force and is transmitted to the ministries and the regional economic administrators. Each authority prepares working instructions within the realm of its competence and transmits the plan with instructions to the lower echelons.

At the end of the chain of command are the enterprises which are asked to prepare enterprise plans. During the Stalinist period when centralization of command was at its peak, each enterprise was circumscribed by a large number of directives, the most important ones concerning (1) the basic production tasks expressed in (*a*) global value of production in fixed (comparable) prices and factory prices and (*b*) the quantities of the major product; (2) specifications concerning increases in productivity and employment level; (3) material allotment limits; (4) specification of planned cost reduction; and (5) financial limits. Under this system, enterprise planning consisted in finding a solution to the production problem subject to all the planned limits.[8] During the Stalinist period, Polish enterprise plans had to conform to as many as 35 separate indicators. The task of designing an acceptable plan was exceedingly difficult, and no room was left for any economic calculus on the enterprise level.

The multiplication of mandatory indicators is a self-defeating task, since the central authorities are not capable of running comprehensive checks and arriving at an over-all evaluation on the basis of such a mass of data. Since the end of Stalinism, the tendency is to curtail the number of

[8] A case study of planning under the old system is given in Marian Walewski and Józef Marek, *Przykład planu techniczno-przemysłowo-finansowego przedsiębiorstwa przemysłu lekkiego*, Warszawa, Wydawnictwo Przemysłu Lekkiego i Spożywczego, 1957.

indicators and to achieve greater consistency and coordination among them. If the performance fails to conform to the planners' wishes, attempts are made to manipulate available indicators instead of constantly imposing new controls over old ones. Enterprises are also given somewhat more leeway in preparing their plans and the economic calculus finds a place, albeit a very modest one, in the process of enterprise-level planning.

Planning in terms of physical production tasks for individual firms entails the coordination of interfirm flows of goods. The output of each firm must correspond to the input plans of the customer firms. The transfers are handled in all the Soviet-bloc countries through the intermediary of centralized trading agencies. Major products specified in detailed physical plans are earmarked in advance for their destination; product groups described in the plan in terms of global volume, but not in terms of detailed assortment, are dealt with much in the manner of normal wholesaling activity.

To simplify the task of product distribution, product standardization is pushed far. Indeed, in the Soviet Union, production to special order is virtually nonexistent,[9] and there is a strong tendency for each firm to produce special parts in its own shops. In Poland, production for special order has been recently encouraged to increase efficiency, and firms now can subcontract instead of purchasing only through centralized agencies.[10]

[9] M. Razumov, "Nektorye problemy uluchsheniya rukovodstva rabotoi promyshlennykh predpriyatii," *Voprosy ekonomiki*, no. 10, 1960.

[10] Marian Klimczyk, "Kooperacja jako nowy przedmiot spra-

The advance planning of production targets results in considerable inefficiency since many firms are unable to determine with precision their input requirements before the production plans are set. According to Polish estimates, 15 to 20 per cent of the products of the iron and steel industry are mistakenly allocated.[11] Firms estimate their needs only to find that their needs are really quite different, but once the production plans are set, they cannot readily be altered. Firms obtain machines which do not suit their needs or which are even entirely superfluous. The machines then have to be adapted for a use for which they were not originally designed, with consequent efficiency loss.

Decisions about what to produce and what factors to purchase result in a secondary balancing process. Enterprises sign contracts for the delivery of products, and simultaneously attempt to assure themselves of adequate factor or production supplies. Contracts of major items are arranged directly between enterprises. Items of minor importance are purchased and sold through trading agencies.

The determination of output and input mix is a simultaneous process. An enterprise does not know what inputs it needs until it is sure what it will produce, but it cannot be sure it will fill orders unless it has contracts for the necessary inputs. Since the national plan sets goals for individual industries, substitution takes place only within product classes. The allocation relies on a contract-recontract system in which prices play a minimal role and pur-

wozdawczości statystycznej przemysłu," *Wiadomosci Statystyczne*, vol. 5, no. 1, 1960.

[11] Bronisław Blass, "O niektórych zagadnieniach zaopatrzenia fabryk," *Myśl Gospodarcza*, vol. 1, no. 4, 1957.

chasers and suppliers often have to settle for a second best. Indeed, in branches of industry where inputs tend to be specific, substantial losses in efficiency may result.[12]

Enterprise plans and interenterprise contracts deal not only with physical items, but also with financial entities. The control over plan fulfillment likewise has a dual character. To clarify the meaning of the enterprise financial plans and the financial controls over plan fulfillment, it is necessary to back-track and consider the meaning and method of preparation of the national financial plan.

d. Financial Planning

The exchange of goods and services in soviet-type economies is carried out in terms of money. Workers receive wages which they spend on personal needs. Enterprises receive payments (in cash or credit) for the goods and services rendered to the ultimate consumers as well as to other enterprises. The government collects taxes and disburses payments. The similarities of the role which money plays in Soviet-bloc countries and in free-enterprise countries are striking. Yet the differences are even more profound.

In capitalist countries, money gives control over resources

[12] The current procedures of interfirm transactions are described in some detail in a series of booklets destined for factory workers' councils. See in particular B. Sołtysinski, "Zaopatrzenie i gospodarka materiałowa w przedsiębiorstwie przemysłowym," *Biblioteka Rady Robotniczej*, Warszawa, Polskie Wydawnictwa Gospodarcze, 1960, and J. Bengom, "Organizacja zbytu i analiza rynku w przedsiebiorstwie przemysłowym," *ibid.*, no. 10.

and plays an important allocative role. Not so in the Soviet-bloc countries. Here the possession of the means of payment

... is not the only, nor even the most important claim on the products of a nationally owned enterprise. Physical plans and material accounts regulate the quality and quantity of products which can be purchased by individual institutions. In the majority of cases such physical plans even state the name of the supplier.[13]

Financial plans translate physical plans into monetary terms. To the flow of goods and services planned for the economy, there corresponds a flow of planned means of payments. The financial plan allocates monetary resources to personal consumption, collective consumption (administration, defense, public services), and to investment in accordance with the planned physical allocation of resources.

The problem of monetary planning is to supply means of payments in quantities necessary for the fulfillment of physical plan objectives. The principal policy tools—and the principal positions in the financial plan—are money creation, credit creation, and fiscal policy.

The main instruments for fiscal and monetary policy are the state budget and the state bank. The form of the budget as well as the formal organization of the banking system have close counterparts in free enterprise nations. Whereas institutions dealing with physical planning are indigenous to the soviet-type economies for want of any free-enterprise counterpart, financial institutions were taken over from

[13] Władysław Jaworski, *Zarys rozwoju systemu Kredytowego w Polsce Ludowej*, Warszawa, Polskie Wydawnictwa Gospodarcze, 1958, pp. 92–93.

predecessor regimes and adapted to the needs of the soviet-type system:

> As society is transformed into a Socialist pattern, new needs arise in the sphere of financial management. In the construction or reconstruction of financial institutions there is a tendency to rely on traditional tools, i.e., on institutions which have been known and tried in the past.[14]

The state budgets of the Soviet-bloc countries contain all the usual items of government receipt and expenditure which appear in the state budgets of free-enterprise countries. The major difference lies in the financing of investments through the budget. The policy implications of budgetary planning are, however, different in free-enterprise and Soviet-bloc countries.

In free-enterprise economies the state budget allocates resources in accordance with the wishes of the government. Governments impose taxes to raise resources for collective uses and also to redistribute purchasing power. Public money is spent on government-sponsored or government-supported schemes (defense, schooling, etc.) and also subsidizes individual consumption of selected population groups, such as the unemployed.

In free-enterprise countries, over-all budgetary policy is relied upon with increasing frequency as a macroeconomic tool. Governments are sometimes able to achieve budgetary surpluses in order to check inflation or balance their foreign trade account. Budgetary deficits, a more frequent

[14] Zdzisław Fedorowicz, *Finanse w gospodarce socjalistycznej,* Warszawa, Polskie Wydawnictwa Gospodarcze, 1960, p. 26.

phenomenon, increase the level of employment and stimulate economic growth.

In the soviet-type economies the use of resources is predetermined by the physical plan; the budget is a reflection of the allocative decisions. The macroeconomic effects of budgetary policy are limited, since the real output policy is isolated to a large extent from price policy. Creation of excessive money and credit, be it through the budget or through banks, causes inflationary pressures, however, and the general policy is to balance the budget for the sake of price stability.

The budgetary policy in Soviet-bloc countries strives to achieve monetary stability on the microeconomic level, "by reallocating money stocks which accumulate in the hands of the population and state enterprises in excess of their current needs as determined by government policy on prices and real output." [15] Excess purchasing power is siphoned off by taxes and fed through budgetary expenditures into the sectors in which purchasing power is deficient. Thus fiscal policy is one of the tools used to equilibrate demand with the quantities supplied in accordance with the plan.

The division of financial responsibilities among the state budget, the state bank, and other banking institutions is largely a matter of convenience. Major investments are financed through the budget. Current credits and minor fixed investments are financed by the banks. Over-all money and credit control rests with the state bank, while diverse

---

[15] Donald R. Hodgman, "Soviet Monetary Control through the Banking System," in Gregory Grossman (ed.), *Value and Plan*, Berkeley, Calif., University of California Press, 1960, p. 109.

financial institutions (such as agricultural banks) cater to the needs of individual sectors of the economy.

Banking policy, like budgetary policy, is subordinated to the national physical plan:

In the Capitalist system the money policy pursued by the bank of issue is one of the main tools of government control over the economy. Under Socialist planning, the national plan is such a basic tool. Under those circumstances the main duty of the bank of issue is to manage the monetary affairs in such a way as to facilitate plan fulfillment.[16]

To satisfy the requirements of the plan, banking authorities adjust the supply of money and credit "to the transaction requirements of the economy, taking prices and real flows as given." [17] This policy has been aptly called an "inverted" version of the quantity theory of money. Under the quantity theory the supply of money controls the price level, given the transaction volume. In Soviet practice the supply of money is adjusted to the transaction volume and the price level.

Money in soviet-type economies ought not to play an autonomous role in resource allocation. When resource use is governed by monetary considerations and not by physical plans, allocation does not occur in accordance with the principles of the system, but contrarily to them.[18] Nevertheless, the financial plan is necessary "to maintain cen-

[16] Władysław Jaworski, *op. cit.*, pp. 92–93.
[17] Donald R. Hodgman, *op. cit.*, p. 123.
[18] Włodzimierz Brus, *Ogólne problemy funkcjonowania gospodarki socjalistycznej*, Warszawa, Państwowy Instytut Wydawniczy, 1961, chap. 3, *passim*.

tralized control over classes of decisions whose details are left to the discretion of firms and households." [19]

In the private and cooperative sectors the financial plan plays an important instrumental role. Although the physical plan specifies the output of the cooperative sector and the consumption of households, the government does not directly allocate the resources, but must induce the desired results. For instance, in order to promote investment in agriculture, the Polish government purchases farmers' products at lower-than-market prices and resells them to consumers at market prices. The profit on the transaction is turned back to the farmers in the form of an investment subsidy. Moreover, the prices at which farmers' produce is purchased must be set at levels which will induce the farmers to produce in accordance with physical plans.

Since the incomes of the private and cooperative sectors cannot be rigidly controlled, the government must rely on taxes and subsidies to attain the desired income distribution. Thus without financial planning it would be almost impossible to fit the nonnationalized sectors within the over-all national plan.

Monetary planning is essential as a link between the national sector and the consumers and workers. For instance, if the state decides to appropriate more resources for consumption purposes and less for investment, it is necessary to give the population more purchasing power. The shift of resources must be accompanied by an increase in wage payments relative to the prices of consumer goods. A shift of resources from consumption to investment must be accompanied by a price-wage movement in the opposite

[19] Donald R. Hodgman, *op. cit.*, p. 113.

direction. Since both prices and wages are government-set, the price-wage change must be planned in coordination with the investment-consumption change.

Within the sector of direct national ownership, the financial plan is drawn primarily for control purposes. A peculiar feature of the soviet-type system is that the state bank has the duty "to exercise control over industrial enterprises in order to discover all shortcomings in plan fulfillment." [20]

Each enterprise in the national sector is treated as a quasi-autonomous unit. Transactions among the national enterprises are conducted in terms of set prices through the intermediary of bank credits and debits. A purchase from another enterprise gives rise to a debit item, while sales are credited. Thus the banks have a continuous record of product transfers which take place in the national sector. The system of crediting gives the authorities an excellent signaling device which shows all delays in deliveries and all bottlenecks.

One might claim that the prices at which the transactions within the national sector are carried out are of no importance to the outside world. A parallel may be drawn with transfers within a single capitalist enterprise. The price paid by the General Motors Chevrolet division for bodies made by Fisher Body—also a division of General Motors—is not reflected either in the price of the cars or the wage of the workers. The transfer is a purely formal transaction.

The traditional method of pricing which prevailed in the Soviet Union and in the other countries of the camp until the 1950s consisted in setting very low prices for producer goods products and high prices for consumer goods products. Under this dual pricing scheme, many branches of pro-

[20] Władysław Jaworski, *op. cit.,* p. 93.

ducer goods industries failed to cover their costs and made
"planned deficits." Consumer goods sectors not only covered
their costs but also contributed to "accumulation" through
the payment of transfer taxes which created the desired
spread between wages and consumer goods prices.

While there are no theoretical objections to "dual pricing,"
the scheme has many practical drawbacks. The system is
an open invitation to commit abuses. Products may be
fictitiously sold for investment purposes and the sale reported at the tax-free low price. The same product may in
reality be sold for consumption purposes and the difference
in price pocketed.

More important objections concern the limitation imposed
by dual pricing on financial control. Control is greatly fa-
cilitated when prices are uniform regardless of the destination of the product and when they are set to cover the enterprise costs. When prices are so set, an enterprise which fulfills the physical plan and keeps within the technical norms
will also fulfill the financial plan. If the physical plan is
overfulfilled without much decrease in efficiency, or if efficiency increases, the enterprise will show a profit over and
above the planned amount. Thus the financial results reflect physical plan fulfillment, and profit-linked bonuses provide an incentive for cost saving.

Under dual pricing, enterprises in the producer goods
sector had to meet planned deficits which destroyed the
validity of financial control. A deficit industry increases its
deficit if it surpasses its physical goals. As long as the magnitude of the deficit is taken as an indication of performance,
there is an open invitation to resource wastage.

The dual pricing system is sometimes defended on the

grounds that low prices of capital goods encourage capital accumulation.[21] When producer goods prices are low, a given amount of taxes will pay for a greater amount of producer goods than when producer goods are high. Reasoning of this type is in fact based on an illusion. The real cost of accumulation depends on the value of resources used for investment purposes and not on the arbitrarily fixed prices of such resources. When the artificially lowered prices were used for investment efficiency calculations, the calculus favored the application of capital-intensive techniques. Thus the dual pricing system resulted in an increased demand for capital goods without easing the supply problem.

The difficulties connected with dual pricing led to a series of price reforms, the most radical of which took place in Poland in 1960. Under the new pricing scheme all enterprises pay for their inputs at uniform transfer prices and receive for their outputs uniform factory prices. The factory prices are set so that each branch of the industry is supposed to cover its costs and achieve a planned profit. The transfer price is computed by adding a turnover tax to the factory price. Efficient enterprises make an extra profit for which they are rewarded, while inefficient ones which fail to meet the planned profit rate suffer penalties.

The principle of uniform pricing is modified in practice in two important ways, and the modifications virtually destroy the uniformity.

Since there exist substantial differences in the technological level of various enterprises in the same field, uniform prices would penalize the technologically backward units and reward the technologically advanced ones. The

[21] See Emanuel Winter, "Rozwój systemu finansowego przedsiębiorstw," *Życie Gospodarcze*, no. 26, 1960.

idea behind introducing the profit motive is to reward good management instead of good technology. To compensate for technological differences, enterprises receive (or make) transfer payments; hence, the prices received by all enterprises are not uniform.

A further modification in the uniform price system is caused by differential turnover taxes. One of the purposes of the turnover tax is to achieve equilibrium in the consumer goods market. The supply of consumer goods is set by the policy makers and little regard is paid to demand. To achieve equilibrium between the quantity supplied and the quantity demanded by the public, differential taxes must be applied. Some products put on the consumer market are priced deliberately to achieve as high an accumulation as possible.[22] Other goods, favored for social and political purposes (or sometimes simply as a result of miscalculation), carry very small margins.[23]

[22] In discussing the advisability of developing the chemical industry, E. Szyr stated that, "the great profitability of the consumer goods produced by the chemical industry is a very important fact. A small investment in the production of orlon or of terylene produces textiles which carry a very high price and insure high accumulation. The accumulation thus obtained is an important argument in favor of developing the chemical industry." (*Niektóre problemy rozwoju gospodarki narodowej w latach 1959–65*, Warszawa, Książka i Wiedza, 1959, p. 39.) It is evident that Szyr's emphasis is not on the benefit to consumers which artificial fibers will bring, but on the possibility of increasing the accumulation fund.

[23] For a partial and incomplete listing of turnover taxes, see Janusz Białobrzeski, Marian Donner, Kazimierz Wickowski, *Podatek obrotowy i podatek dochodowy*, Warszawa, Wydawnictwo Prawnicze, 1958. Turnover taxes are frequently changed, and their levels cannot be readily ascertained.

Every national enterprise has its own financial plan which corresponds to its physical plan and is incorporated in the over-all national financial scheme. The enterprise receives a wage fund. The fund has some flexibility, for the exact disbursements depend on the number of workers employed and on the physical output. In general there is a maximum which cannot be surpassed, as well as wage scales which have to be observed.

Wage payments are made by enterprises from funds obtained through commercial operations. Receipts are credited to the bank account, and cash drawn from the bank for wage payments is debited. The working capital needs of the enterprises are covered by a line of credit which is either interest-free or carries a nominal interest. The amount of working capital needed by each enterprise is estimated on the basis of financial "norms." These norms reflect the length of the production period, the periodicity of factor supply, the periodicity of demand for products, etc. The financial norms are thus derived from the physical norms which show the allowable input needs per unit of output. Unlike the physical norms, the financial norms are couched in global terms, and do not deal with specific details of the production process.

The normal bank credits cover only the planned working capital needs. When extraordinary needs arise, special credits may be granted. The granting of special credits gives the banks an opportunity to scrutinize the enterprise management. It may turn out, for instance, that an enterprise needs special credits because it fails to deliver its products according to schedule. If the fault lies with the management, the bank may charge interest on the credits. The interest diminishes the planned profit and adversely affects the managerial bonus.[24]

The financial plan of the individual national enterprise consists of the wage fund, a schedule of prices at which transactions are to take place, financial norms, taxes to be paid, and credit limits. In the aggregate, these entities are included in the national financial plan, but do not exhaust the plan. To the wage disbursements made by public enterprises, one must add wage disbursements made by the administration and cooperative and private producers. To the turnover tax plan, one must add profit and income taxes paid by the sectors which are not under direct national ownership. The credit plan must also include credits to the other sectors.

The financial plan in its entirety thus includes the national budget, the national credit plan, and a detailed finan-

[24] During Poland's Six-Year-Plan period all normal credits granted to nationalized industry carried a 2 per cent interest rate. Credits which had to be extended beyond the period foreseen by the financial plan carried a 4 per cent rate. Producer's cooperative, at that time much favored as a transitional form from private enterprise, could borrow at 1 per cent. Large farmers and private industry were charged 8 per cent on loans, and small farmers 5 per cent. Thus it will be seen that the credit policy was used as a tool favoring preferred modes of organization, and as a performance control. (See K. Neumann, "Stopa procentowa w Polsce w latach 1945–1958," *Narodowy Bank Polski, Wiadomości*, vol. 16, no. 3, p. 131, 1960.) It must be noted that the levels of interest were so low that the differentials were made virtually insignificant. Outright refusal to grant credit, and even more, direct physical action, were the main policy tools, while the importance of interest rate policy was not significant.

cial plan for the national sector. In Western terms the financial plan is a combination budget, cash flow analysis, and projected profit and loss statement for all the enterprises taken as a whole. The plan is a document of immense complexity, and a modicum of simplicity is achieved only through the use of very broad aggregates.

The financial plan should in theory be an exact replica of the physical plan. The sheer magnitude of the task of preparing two plans, as well as conceptual differences, explains why the two plans do not correspond to each other in practice.

The physical plan deals with physical entities, such as consumer goods, producer goods, and social consumption goods and services. The aggregates are formed by using fixed (comparable) prices. The financial plan works in terms of a wage fund, an accumulation fund (divided into investment and other purposes), and credit. The aggregates are formed with the aid of financial (transfer and factory) prices. These do not bear a constant relation to the fixed (comparable) prices. Thus every time a new plan is drawn, all the price concepts have to be retranslated. Further modifications must be made as institutions are modified. To use one example: If it is decided that some investments which used to be included in the budget ought to be financed through the enterprise funds, it is necessary to change the budget, the enterprise funds, the taxes levied upon enterprises, and possibly also the credits to enterprises—even if the physical plan is not modified in any way.

Discrepancies between the fulfillment of physical and financial plans are almost inevitable, even if the two plans happen to coincide. One or two illustrations will suffice to explain the nature of the problem. Assume that the physical plan is overfulfilled. If the overfulfillment occurs only in the producer goods industries, there is an increase in wages (which are linked to physical output) without a corresponding increase in consumer goods, hence the balance of the consumer goods market is destroyed. If the overfulfillment occurs in consumer goods industries, the imbalance in the consumer goods market does not necessarily arise. On the other hand, the "accumulation" margin of the consumer goods production is generally quite high, so there is an increase in the accumulation in financial means without a corresponding increase in the output of producer goods.

In all the soviet-type economies, only the physical plans have a directive force. Since the physical and financial plans often diverge, it is impossible for both types to have a directive meaning. The primacy goes to the physical plans which reflect the quantitative decisions of the policy makers. The physical plans also allocate unambiguously the individual tasks. The financial plans, by contrast, are "synthetic" to use the Soviet parlance. They deal with global entities, and their fulfillment depends upon the cooperation of diverse elements. Thus, the financial plans are prepared as a check, not as a rule for action.

e. Plan Fulfillment Control

Physical as well as financial methods are used for purposes of control of economic activity. To manage the economy through directives, the policy makers must keep in constant touch with the operational level. Short-term plans are often issued with considerable delay and in the interim

period the economy must be managed by *ad hoc* orders.[25]
Even when a plan is in force, it is necessary to check on
its fulfillment, to issue additional orders, and to gather information for subsequent planning.

A preliminary appraisal of plan execution is prepared in
Poland by the Central Planning Commission every ten days.
For this report the Commission gathers data on the volume
of money in circulation, wages paid out, inventories of consumer goods, and the volume of interenterprise transactions.

A comprehensive report on the state of the economy is
issued by the Planning Commission on a monthly basis.
This report gives data on physical plan fulfillment, as well
as on financial affairs. It discusses the major problems facing
the economy and makes recommendations for corrective
action.

The monthly report contains balances of the most important entities, such as employment, basic raw materials,
foreign trade, and consumer goods. Explanations are provided for departures from the planned balances and forecasts of future developments.

Ordinarily the bulk of the monthly report is devoted to
a discussion of industrial developments. Changes in the
volume of interenterprise transfers, the raw material situation, and the availability of power are watched and com-
mented upon. The report appraises changes in inventory
levels and in the supply of industrial consumer goods.

[25] Short-term plans covering the calendar year are often issued in April or even later. Some observers conclude, therefore,
that the plans are meaningless. This is not so; since plans are
largely an extrapolation of past trends, enterprises may readily
anticipate the plan by extrapolation of past orders. Major
changes in short-term plans are antedated by government directives which give the enterprises a clue to the future plans.

Since the agricultural sector in Poland remains largely under private ownership, the verification of plan fulfillment necessarily has a somewhat different character than in the other sectors. The information given in the monthly bulletin concentrates on the agricultural sector's demand for city goods, as well as on the supply of goods to the city. Most of the important agricultural commodities are sold through State trading agencies on the basis of long-term contracts, and the reports show the degree of fulfillment of the contracts. Special attention is paid to the agricultural sector's purchases of fertilizers and machinery.

Under the current Polish scheme a substantial proportion of investment is under the jurisdiction of regional authorities, trusts, and cooperatives; hence, a periodic control of the volume of investment is essential for the preservation of over-all equilibrium. The monthly report shows the accumulation of financial means for investment purposes, the volume of investments undertaken, and the structure of investment expenditures. Delays in the completion of investment projects are signaled. On the basis of such information, measures are taken to freeze investment funds if needed to preserve over-all financial balance or to set up priority schemes where bottlenecks appear.

Every monthly report contains information on foreign trade movements. Here again, observed deviations from the plan are utilized to issue proper directives. Finally, data are given on personal incomes, the level of consumer prices, and retail trade turnover.

The monthly reports of the Commission are discussed in detail by the Presidium of the Commission, which transmits its recommendation to the government. If the government agrees with the Commission's diagnosis, appropriate direc-

tives are issued. These directives sometimes modify certain
provisions of the national plan, but more often they concern issues which the plan left for lower-level determination. Whenever practice shows that the decisions reached
at lower administrative levels are inimical to the over-all
plan fulfillment, corrective directives are issued by the government.

Throughout the year the government issues directives in
response to the information obtained from the periodic reports. The directives correct mistakes which crept into the
plans and in plan execution and handle contingencies which
were not foreseen when the plan was drawn. Direct orders
also often deal with matters which were originally left to
lower echelons. Thus the *ad hoc* directives increase the degree of centralized control over and above the central orders
contained in the Plan.

The *ad hoc* directives remedy individual defects in the
system. Whether or not they have a salubrious long-run
effect is an open matter. By masking defects, directives may
delay the introduction of needed fundamental reforms.
Moreover, where directives are superimposed on incentives,
neither the directive system nor the incentive system may
work satisfactorily. At this point these issues are signaled
briefly; they will be debated in more detail in the next
chapter, when we shall consider the economy in action.

f. Short-term Planning—Problems and Difficulties

The short-term planning method employed in the soviet-
type economies relies on the cooperation of the various

levels in the economy and on a method of successive approximations. The policy makers give the first directives for the construction of the plan and approve the final project. The planning technicians translate the first directives into tasks specified in the indicators. Enterprises, trusts, and ministries elaborate the projects which in turn are coordinated and made into a draft national plan presented to the leadership. Finally, the plan is modified in the light of the leadership's desires and put into a final form by the technicians.

Under the multilevel scheme each level is supposed to contribute the information within the sphere of its competence. The political leadership is competent (by definition) to make the basic decisions on the direction of development. This information is transmitted to the planners who have special competence in the drafting of an over-all plan. The economic administrators and the enterprises utilize the information contributed by the policy makers and the planners and contribute their specialized knowledge of actual production processes. The second phase of planning utilizes the information gathered at the operating levels to correct the initial indicators. The draft plan gives new information to the policy makers, who once more make over-all decisions, and these are finally modified and coordinated by the planners.

In the multilevel planning process some confusion arises between information and directives. Are the indicators supposed to provide a general framework for detailed planning or are they an order which the lower levels should accept? If the former is true, then each enterprise should outline its individual plan and should explore all the possibilities of development, using the indicators much in the manner in which a capitalist enterprise uses a market forecast. If the latter is true then the enterprise ought to specify in detail the inputs and outputs consistent with the indicators. In the former case, the enterprise takes an active part in the process of planning. In the latter, it merely performs calculations in accordance with the rules laid out by the Planning Commission.

The lack of clarity concerning the role of indicators is seen in the criticism voiced against enterprise-level planning. In the opinion of a high official of the Polish Planning Commission:

> The indicators issued by the Council of Ministers to serve as a basis for the elaboration of the National Economic Plan are the result of prolonged studies carried out by the Planning Commission and the Ministry of Finance in cooperation with the economic ministries. The indicators are then carefully analyzed by the economic committee attached to the Council of Ministers and by the Council of Ministers itself.[26]

The implication of this statement is that the indicators are an authoritative expression of planning purpose. Enterprise planning ought to consist of giving itemized lists of inputs and outputs consistent with the indicators. In reality, officials at the operational level tamper with the indicators and force through readjustments.

Concurrently with complaints that the lower echelons do not take the indicators seriously enough, complaints are

[26] Stefan Hatt, "Pierwsze wnioski z resortowych projektów planów na rok 1960," *Gospodarka Planowa*, vol. 14, no. 10, p. 1, 1959.

heard that planning is nothing more than an elaboration of the initial indicators. The tendency to perform mechanical manipulations and to call them planning is especially strong on the enterprise level:

> Planning on the enterprise level is identified in a very concrete fashion with the forms on the basis of which the plan is elaborated and with the method of filling the forms.[27]

The two types of complaints are inconsistent, yet they are readily understandable. By modifying the indicators, enterprises distort the carefully devised scheme of the Planning Commission; but by adhering slavishly to the indicators, enterprises deprive the Commission of valuable information on production possibilities.

The multilevel scheme of planning is based on the assumption that all the participants in planning have the same aims. In so far as this is not true (in so far as there is a conflict of goals), the modifications made by the planners and the operating level may run counter to the interests represented by policy makers. Conflicts of interest transform planning by successive approximation into planning by bargaining and compromise.

The dual nature of soviet-type planning is also a source of difficulties and conflicts. The physical plan reckons output in physical units and forms aggregates in terms of constant weights. The physical plan sets enterprise goals in physical terms, and enterprise performance is judged in terms of such goals. The physical plan relies on factory and

[27] Michał Malicki, "Uwagi o systemie planowania," *Gospodarka Planowa*, vol. 14, no. 11, p. 22, 1960.

transfer prices, and controls the economy in terms of inter-enterprise financial transactions. The financial plan gives profit incentives to enterprises and rewards financial performance. The subordination of the financial plan to the physical plan does not solve the conflict between goals and incentives, but merely assigns them relative weights.

g. Summary and Conclusions

Short-term plans provide detailed blueprints which govern the activities of the economy during the planned year. Plans indicate what each enterprise is to produce and what inputs it is to utilize. For the cooperative and private sector (if any), planning is less detailed, but such sectors, too, are given tasks and are assigned the means to carry out these tasks.

The consistency of plans is ensured through material balancing. Groups of commodities and individual commodities are balanced so that the planned supply is equal to the sum of the planned uses. Inputs necessary to produce the planned output are calculated on the basis of technological norms. To achieve an over-all consistency of the plan, input flows are adjusted to satisfy the production requirements. The solution, obtained through iterations, is approximate. In fact, there is usually little time for a careful balancing of the final version of the plan.

Short-term planning virtually ignores the problem of efficient resource use. The reliance on input norms and the strict rationing of deficit commodities are merely makeshift devices. No attempt is made to arrive at a consistent ranking of scarcities. Such a ranking requires the expression of qualitatively different entities in common terms, and the assignment of scarcity values to all commodities. Once such values (or prices) are assigned, allocation proceeds according to an input minimization-output maximization rule. This procedure is not followed by soviet-type planning, where the allocation of resources is made in physical terms prior to the assignment of prices and values. As a consequence no general principle of economizing applies.

Every short-term plan has a financial plan counterpart. The financial plan provides the producing units and the consumers with the means of payments necessary to carry out the tasks specified in the financial plan at fixed prices. Financial planning imposes plan discipline on sectors of the economy which cannot be subject to detailed physical controls. It also facilitates current performance control and encourages "economizing" at the factory level.

Financial plans should, in theory, correspond exactly to the physical plans, as a translation of physical plan targets into value terms. In fact discrepancies between the two types of plans are almost inevitable. The physical plan is built upwards from individual output targets and input requirements; the financial plan, on the other hand, starts with broad requirements for new money and credit issues and with broad macroeconomic aggregates. Since the planning process involves many rough approximations, the two types of plans never quite agree with each other.

The duality of planning creates conflicts in the soviet-type economies which are not known in the free-enterprise system. Under free enterprise the profit motive is the guide for private economic activity. Under soviet-type planning an enterprise is supposed to pursue physical goals as well as financial goals. When the two fail to coincide, the enterprise is guided and propelled by two different sets of considerations. Thus, paradoxically, though soviet-type planning is supposed to ensure the unity of purpose of all economic activity, it fails to present its plans in an integrated fashion. To what extent this lack of integration prevents the achievement of the leadership's goals and how enterprises function under the intricate system of directives and incentives is discussed in Chapter 6.

6

The Soviet-type Economy
in Operation

The stage is now set for a discussion of the operation of a soviet-type economy. The directive short-term plan gives a unified purpose of action for the whole economy. The problem is how to enforce the plan and how to make the diverse productive units cooperate in the fulfillment of national goals.

a. Economic Conflicts in a "Conflict-free" System

If the theory of the conflict-free socialist society were correct, plan enforcement would be a simple matter. The national economic plan represents the unitary interests of the whole nation, hence all the productive units should

181

strive to fulfill their portion of the plan. Once the tasks are allotted by the central authorities, enforcement is automatic. Mistakes in execution could arise if the plan were not properly designed or if the producing units misinterpreted their assignments, but there would be no need to provide sanctions and incentives to fulfill the tasks. The entire problem would be reduced to the problem of correct planning and of adequate information transmission.

From the earliest days of the Soviet system it was evident that the unitary purpose is a fiction: To fulfill plans, it is necessary to give inducements to the productive units, that is, to give them incentives over and above those provided by national interest. Since Stalin's death it is even permissible to discuss freely the conflicts of goals in a soviet-type society:

It is possible to posit that the satisfaction of the needs of society is the direct motive for action of the central authorities, especially in the field of investment. Such a stand is only partially justified if one regards the motivation of state enterprises.[1]

Where the interests of the various sectors of society do not coincide, the over-all national goal must be replaced by individual goals. The problem then arises how the various individual goals are to be coordinated in order to serve the national purpose represented by the plan.

Let us take one step back and consider whether the national plan really represents the national purpose. The plan is prepared jointly by the political leaders, planning tech-

[1] Ber Haus and Przemysław Kotlarek, "Cel gospodarki socjalistycznej a cel przedsiębiorstwa," *Gospodarka Planowa*, vol. 15, no. 12, p. 26, 1960.

nicians, and economic administrators. The success of the Party is measured by the tangible economic achievements. The Party is interested in mobilizing plans which prod the individuals and enterprises to a maximum effort and propel the economy forward. The operative units will have to carry out the plan, and their success is measured in terms of plan fulfillment and overfulfillment. A very taut plan increases the difficulty of reaching the goals. Hence the enterprises (and to a lesser extent the higher economic administrators) are interested in plans which can easily be met. The planners' interests are somewhat different: Planners are technicians, and their competence is measured by the exactitude of a plan. If the operations of the economy conform to the plan, the plan is a success. If the plan is overfulfilled or underfulfilled by a wide margin, it is improperly drawn.

The preliminary indicators issued by the planning office at the beginning of the planning process represent the political leadership's wishes as tempered by the planning technicians' judgment. The draft projects prepared by enterprises on the basis of the indicators introduce modifications in line with the enterprise interests. The economic ministries which aggregate and modify enterprise projects occupy an intermediate position between the top political leadership and the operative level of the economy. As members of the policy-making group, the top administrators wish to promote rapid development. As administrators, they want to show how well the branch of industry under their control can fulfill its assigned tasks. As a consequence at the ministerial level, the plans drawn by the enterprises are made more taut; nevertheless, they are likely to represent a downward revision of the preliminary indicators:

The materials and plan projects sent back by the ministries
show in general a low rate of production growth, a higher index
of employment growth, a lower index of productivity growth
and a higher index of investment than the preliminary indicators.[2]

In the preparation of the final plan the ministerial estimates are revised upward by the Planning Commission, and
a further upward revision is made in the course of the political reviewing of the draft plan. Sometimes, as in 1958,
the final result is less taut than the preliminary indicators,
as shown in Table 6.

*Table 6   Comparisons of the initial indices for the Polish plan
for 1958 with the final version of the plan
(1957 = 100)*

	Preliminary indicators	Final plan
Value of the global product of nationalized industry	108.0	107.2
Value of material production	108.3	107.8
Employment in nationalized industry and administration	103.6	104.7
Wage fund	105.0	105.2
Costs of production as per cent of value of production of the nationalized sector	81.3	82.4

Source: Stefan Hatt, "Pierwsze wnioski z resortowych projektów
planów na rok 1960," *Gospodarka Planowa,* vol. 14, no. 10, 1959, p. 1.

It is clear from Table 6 that the final tasks are less onerous
than the tasks set by the indicators, while the employment

[2] E. Szyr's speech at the 12th Plenum of the Central Committee of the PZPR, Warsaw, 1958 (mimeographed).

level, the wage fund and the costs of production per unit output are higher.

Comparisons of the actual performance with the preliminary indicators and the final plan show who has the upper hand in the bargaining process. During the period from 1955 to 1958 the Polish leadership made efforts not to alienate the workers, and the corrections introduced by the operating level were taken into account, sometimes against the better judgment of the planners. Results show that the indicators were a better appraisal of actual production possibilities than the final plans (see Table 7).

Table 7 Comparison of preliminary indicators, final plans, and actual plan performance in Poland, 1957 and 1958

	Preliminary indicator	Plan	Actual production
Global product 1958 as % of global product in 1957 (in 1958 prices)	107.2	106.1	109.5
Global product 1959 as % of global product in 1958 (in 1959 prices)	109.3	107.4	109.4

Source: Stefan Hatt, "Pierwsze wnioski z resortowych projektów planów na rok 1960," *Gospodarka Planowa*, vol. 14, no. 10, 1959, p. 3.

There is, of course, no reason to believe that the actual performance will always conform more closely to the indicators than to the final plan. If the indicators are initially too ambitious, the subsequent modifications bring them closer to a feasible level. Moreover, if the policy makers' preferences change between the preparation of the indicators and the final revision of the plan, the ultimate plan figures may be higher than the indicators. Whatever the final outcome, the process of planning is a bargaining process. The outcome depends on the relative strength and skill of the parties. One is free to define the final result as "national interest," but one must realize that the plan is molded by opposing goals and tendencies.

In the bargaining over the national plan enterprises seek to ease their tasks by exaggerating the input requirements and by playing down the output potential. These tendencies are combatted by the economic administrators and by the planners through the imposition of production norms. These norms, as we have seen, are based in part on technical calculations and in part on statistical observation of actual performance.

Norms are designed to reflect "average superior performance." Norms should be feasible, yet they should be sufficiently taut to elicit an effort on the part of the enterprise. How to discover the proper degree of tautness is a major problem for planners in Soviet-bloc countries.

When norms are steadily being surpassed by most or even all the enterprises in a given field, they are adjusted upward, since a readily surpassable norm does not serve its purpose. For instance, in the first half of 1955 the coal-loading operations in the Stettin harbor surpassed all norms by 60 to 150 per cent. As a consequence new norms were imposed during the preparation of the next plan.[3]

The correction of norms in keeping with actual perform-

[3] Zbigniew Heliński, "Analiza norm wydajności pracy przy przeładunku węgla w porcie Szczecińskim," *Przegląd Statystyczny*, vol. 7, no. 2, 1960.

ance is not an isolated incident. At the 3d Congress of the Polish United Workers' Party, Gomułka observed that:

In several branches of industry the role of norms has been distorted. The principle according to which norms express the amount of socially essential labor has been violated. According to September 1958 data, norm fulfillment in the metal-working industry equals some 200 per cent. Depending upon the establishment, the degree of norm fulfillment varies from 113 per cent to 340 per cent.[4]

Needless to say, such an observation coming from a top Party leader is a prelude to norm readjustment.

If norms are not being overfulfilled, one cannot conclude that the norms represent good production levels. Although an enterprise might have a hoard of labor and excessive capacity, it might be careful not to overfulfill its targets for fear of receiving more difficult assignments. To take such an enterprise's statement of capacity at face value is to give waste a seal of approval.

To detect misstatements in enterprise plans, economic administrators occasionally make surveys investigating the production processes and enterprise plans. For instance, a survey conducted by the Polish Ministry of Heavy Industry shows that in heavy industry the planned inputs of nonferrous metals were 37 per cent higher than needed for production and normal inventory purposes.[5]

[4] W. Gomułka's speech at the *3d Congress of PZPR, op. cit.,* p. 99.

[5] Jerzy Kopiński, "Podniesienie jakości produkcji—ważny problem gospodarczy," *Gospodarka Planowa,* vol. 14, no. 6, p. 6, 1959.

The spot checks made by economic administrators are not to be taken as an unbiased appraisal of needs. The surveys consider normal needs. They do not take into account the fact that excessive input planning is a form of insurance against nondelivery. When plans are taut, nondelivery or delivery of defective inputs is a frequent occurrence. To prevent interruptions in the production process, one must plan with a safety margin. Since excessive input planning is costless to the enterprises, the safety margin tends to be very large. On the other hand, administrative surveys are conducted on the assumption that the economy works without breakdowns. Economic interests of the nation require the weighing of inventory costs against the cost of interruptions in production. The actual input level permitted by the plan is not the result of the calculation but of a bargaining process in which one party wishes to maximize inputs and the other to minimize them.

Whatever the final plan for inputs and outputs, enterprises have a second chance to ensure themselves against stoppages of work. When interenterprise contracts are concluded, there is a tendency to contract for the purchase of inputs over and above the planned needs and also to promise delivery over and above the planned capacity. The excessive input contracts can be cancelled at little or no extra cost should deliveries be made on time. Within limits such excess contracts do little harm, though in some cases (as in the construction industry) they may lead to unforeseen delay in the completion of projects demanding the cooperation of diverse enterprises.

Investment planning, as distinct from current input planning, is also subject to a form of multilateral bargaining. Long-term investments are discussed by the economic ministries and the political authorities, with ministries fighting for large allotments and the political authorities keeping the demands in check. Where the expansion or modernization of existing enterprises is concerned, the enterprise managements also enter the battle.

The need for enterprise enlargement or modernization is discussed within the framework of long-term as well as short-term plans. Enterprises state their investment requirements in the annual draft projects and also in longer-term enterprise plans which are now coming into fashion. Investment needs also come to light in the course of balancing. Where capacities are insufficient to meet output demand, expansion must be undertaken unless direct factor allocation is resorted to.

Except for small improvements made out of the enterprise funds (and known as "decentralized investments") all investments are financed through nonreturnable interest-free budgetary allotment. As long as an investment facilitates the meeting of a production goal, it is costless to the enterprise. Hence every enterprise has every inducement to demonstrate the need for investment and very little reason to calculate the efficiency of investment. The same holds true for regional and local authorities which receive budgetary allocations of investment funds.

All the investment projects are subject to dual scrutiny: They are examined by the respective ministries and by the planners for the physical production effects, and they are checked by the financial authorities. Since the number of projects presented always exceeds the available financial means, there is a tendency to reject costly projects or trim them down.

The scrutiny of investment plans leads to the rejection of many useless projects, but it also favors misrepresentation. A project which makes high claims for the physical results and presents a modest financial estimate is likely to gain acceptance. There is a premium on misrepresentation. An honest project is less likely to get accepted than one which makes plausible though false claims.[6] Once the project is started, it often turns out that the financial estimates were too modest. Unless additional funds are granted, the investment might go entirely to waste; hence, there is pressure to grant more funds. The practice known as "getting a toehold on the plan" is quite widespread.

Although there is no systematic compendium comparing initial investment cost estimates with the actual investment costs, case studies show that halving the estimated costs is not an unusual occurrence.[7] Moreover:

> Although undoubtedly it would be possible to find contrary examples [i.e., cases in which actual costs were lower than the preliminary estimates] one can say with full certainty that estimates of costs are in general extremely inaccurate, and that there is a tendency to understate costs.[8]

[6] See Mieczysław Jaslar, "Przyczynek do dyskusji o roli finansów w gospodarce narodowej," *Finanse,* vol. 10, no. 8, 1959, *passim.*

[7] See Juliusz Kargol, "Zaangażowanie dochodu narodowego w działalności inwestycyjnej," *Finanse,* vol. 11, no. 2, 1960, pp. 54–60.

[8] *Ibid.,* p. 56.

As a consequence of underestimating investment costs, there is a constant pressure to increase investments over and above the planned level. In the second half of 1959, for instance, the planned investment had to be supplemented by an additional 2.2 billion złotys, that is, by some 8 per cent.[9]

In a full employment regime, increases in investment above the planned level necessitate cutbacks in consumer goods production below the planned level. The system of budgetary allotment for investment funds generates a constant pressure for more investment. Here we have one of the paradoxes of the soviet-type economy. The political leadership clearly has a greater preference for investment than the consumers, yet in the operation of the system, the political authorities must stem the flood of demands for investments, in order to maintain consumer goods production.

The strategy of "getting a toehold on the plan" leads to a broad front of investment project starts. Even if additional funds are later voted, excessive starts run into capacity barriers, with consequent delays in the completion of projects. In a free-enterprise economy, delays in completion are a cost to the enterprise which has to pay interest on the invested funds, but in a soviet-type economy, the investment funds are provided interest free. Therefore, waiting is costless to the unit responsible for the investment project. Indeed, the cost of waiting does not appear explicitly in any of the calculations. The consequences are quite startling: in 1959 the estimated cost of investment projects in process

[9] A. Szerwentka, "Polityka inwestycyjna w roku 1959 i najważniejsze zadania planu inwestycyjnego na rok 1960," *Gospodarka Planowa*, vol. 15, no. 12, 1960.

was approximately equal to the annual national product.[10]

In recent years the false claims concerning investment projects and the delays in completion have caused serious alarm. To remedy the situation, stringent controls are being introduced. As of 1960, additional investment funds are granted only in unusual circumstances, and units presenting inadequate or distorted investment plans are subject to penalties. The new regulations [11] may mitigate some of the difficulties, but they do not solve the basic problem. As long as capital is provided cost-free, the number of projects presented must exceed the number of projects accepted. Hence, there must be rationing. Unless the central authorities stand ready to scrutinize all the investment plans in detail, allocation will remain capricious, and the enterprise or administrative unit which presents its case in the most persuasive manner is the most likely to gain approval for its project, regardless of the inherent merits.

The investment plans as well as the operative national plan represent a compromise, not a consensus. The divergence of interests does not disappear with the moment of plan adoption, and it is necessary to induce the individual units to conform to the plan.

b. Plan Enforcement: Directives and Incentives

Plan enforcement can be secured either through direct order or indirect inducement. Soviet-type economies rely on

[10] Rada Ekonomiczna przy Radzie Ministrów, *Sytuacja gospodarcza kraju w roku 1959*, Warszawa, Polskie Wydawnictwa Gospodarcze, 1960, pp. 97ff.

[11] See T. Dietrich, "Budżet PRL na rok 1960," *Finanse*, vol. 11, no. 2, 1960, pp. 10ff.

both methods, though the relative importance attached to directives as against inducements varies over time:

> There is no uniform method, and there cannot be a uniform method, for combining central directives with incentives influencing indirectly the decentralized decisions. No single method can be applicable under all circumstances and to all problems. It is therefore necessary to resort to a variety of solutions and to tailor the solutions to the problems.[12]

Directives issued by the central authority were the main tool of plan enforcement during the Stalinist period, though even then indirect inducements played a substantial role. In the early days of the Soviet regime in Russia and again in the recent period, indirect inducements have received greater emphasis.

A system which relies primarily on centralized directives must develop a method for rapid transmission of detailed orders from the central authority to the operative units and of performance information from the operative units to the central authority. In the limiting case the operative unit is powerless to undertake any action without central sanction. The only stimulus to which the operative unit reacts is the central order:

> Under the centralized system it was assumed that it is possible to transmit to the central authorities all the information concerning the productive possibilities of all the enterprises. As a consequence, the central plan had to be sufficiently detailed to outline all the operations within the economy. There was a tendency to build plans on the basis of individual norms of performance and on norms of exploitation of the diverse

[12] Z. Fedorowicz, *Finanse w gospodarce socjalistycznej*, Warszawa, Polskie Wydawnictwa Gospodarcze, 1960, p. 23.

types of industrial installations. As a consequence, administration of enterprises concentrated on the fulfillment of the technical and economic norms. The role of the individual administrators in the improvement of the plan disappeared, while the single planning office had the increasingly difficult task of working out detailed individual technical norms for all the enterprises.[13]

A system which relies primarily on centralized directives leads to a proliferation of directives. Imagine that initially the directive issued to a multiproduct enterprise is limited to a global number expressing the aggregate physical output target. The enterprise which receives such a directive will generally seek to fulfill its task in the easiest fashion. The minimization of effort will take place in terms of the the product transformation possibilities and the weights used in arriving at the global output goal. The technological possibilities of substituting one kind of output for other kinds determine the opportunity costs of the various products, while the aggregates used in determining the goal are the output prices.

If the central authorities' preferences do not coincide with the enterprise minimum effort calculations, enterprises must be instructed to change their output mix. Hence, added directives are needed to specify output details. The process of specification continues until output is completely specified. Much the same process of increasing specification occurs on the input side, until all input details are specified.[14]

The more detailed the directives, the greater the rigidity

[13] Włodzimierz Hagemajer, "Agregacja a planowanie," *Ekonomista*, no. 6, p. 33, 1958.

[14] For an account of the directives which enterprises had to follow in the Soviet Union, see Y. A. Kronrod, *Osnovy khoziaistvennogo roscheta*, Moscow, 1952, pp. 31ff.

of the system. The system implies a complete rigidity in the policy makers' preferences as to output levels. If one line of output comes to a halt, the factors cannot be transferred to any other kind of production, but must stand idle.

The system of directives aims at a concentration of control on the central administrative level, but the proliferation of directives weakens control. As more and more information reaches the central level, checking for accuracy and processing becomes increasingly difficult. There is strong reason to believe that at the zenith of the directive planning period the central authorities had very little information on the state of the economy. By having to report on every step, enterprises could fake reports and escape detection. Since it is always easier to report success than to achieve it, paper performance of the economy was excellent, but no one, and least of all the supervisory authorities, knew the real state of affairs.

In the period of detailed directive planning, incentives were meant as a reward for acting in accordance with the plan and not as indications of goals other than those given in the plan. If an enterprise failed to fulfill the production plan by more than a given percentage (usually 2 per cent or 5 per cent), the management and the white-collar workers received no bonus.[15] For performance which surpassed the plan, substantial bonuses were paid. In 1957 bonuses paid to white-collar workers in Poland averaged 34 per cent of the base pay in the construction industry and as much as 85 per cent in heavy industry.[16]

[15] See Polska Akademia Nauk, Zakład Nauk Ekonomicznych, *Z prac Zakładu Nauk Ekonomicznych*, no. 2, 1956.
[16] Halina Diamand, *O polityce*, Warszawa, Książka i Wiedza, 1958, p. 44.

Since performance was measured in terms of the degree
of fulfillment of the physical plan, the maximization of the
ratio of the actual performance to the planned performance
became a goal in itself. Notwithstanding the theoretical
scheme:

> Since the basis for bonus payments was the volume of output
> determined by the plan and not an invariant reference point
> such as the level of output, there was a tendency to lower the
> planned goals and to hide the production potential. After the
> goals were fixed, management concentrated on surpassing the
> plan indices, often without attention to the economic results.[17]

Plan fulfillment was reckoned in terms of gross output;
hence, the management's objective was to maximize the
gross output of the enterprise by concentrating on items
with a high material input content. As long as product-mix
changes were permitted, products with a high value added
by manufacturing were likely to be neglected or, whenever
possible, subcontracted. Moreover, as long as financial results did not influence managerial pay, little attention was
paid to the cost of production or to the quality of products.
Even though penalties were levied for the violation of
financial norms and for substandard production, it was ad-
vantageous to pay the fines and concentrate on the level
of output.

There is ample (though anecdotal) evidence that the
visible waste under the directive system of planning was
one of the main reasons for increased reliance on incentives
in the post-Stalinist period. The illustrations given here

[17] *Ibid.*, pp. 43–44.

cover a sufficiently wide range of industries to show that the problem of waste was extremely serious.

Losses attributable to substandard production have been estimated by one writer to equal 1 to 2 per cent of Poland's national product.[18] This figure seems to be extremely low, though no precise estimates can be made. A 1958 control survey showed that 30 per cent of the butter samples and 38 per cent of the cheese samples were substandard.[19] In the production of radios covered by a one-year guarantee, between 16 and 29 per cent of the radios were returned because of factory defects.[20] Twenty-one per cent of the cotton goods produced in 1953 in Łodz, Poland's largest and long-established textile center, was defective.[21]

The situation was not much better in the high-priority heavy industry. Thirty-four per cent of Poland's iron castings and 61 per cent of the nonferrous castings were defective.[22] Even in export industries, it is not rare for 25 per cent or more of the output to be rejected.

Losses due to delays in deliveries are no less serious. In the Soviet Union the over-all idle time resulting from material shortages and poor work coordination is estimated at 20 per cent of the total working time.[23] In Poland the most

[18] Jerzy Kopiński, *op. cit.*

[19] *Ibid.*

[20] *Ibid.*

[21] Speech of Jan Jabłoński at the 2d Congress of the PZPR reported in *Biuletyn II Zjazdu PZPR,* IV dzień obrad, Warszawa, March, 1954, p. 35.

[22] L. Gluck, "Zagadnienie zapasów w gospodarce narodowej," *Narodowy Bank Polski, Wiadomości,* vol. 14, no. 2, p. 61, 1959.

[23] M. Kabaj, "Mechanizm zatrudnienia w gospodarce so-cjalistycznej," *Ekonomista,* no. 1, pp. 52ff., 1960. Kabaj bases

efficient rolling mills are idle 20 per cent of the time, and the average for the whole industry is 39 per cent.[24]

Since the figures chosen by critics are likely to be exceptional, one should refrain from striking an over-all average. The losses are great enough, however, to explain the assiduity with which visible waste is currently attacked.

Throughout the Stalinist period, direct orders played the role of the main policy tool, and incentives were considered a method of order enforcement. When incentives produced results contrary to the orders, more orders were issued. In the post-Stalinist period the orientation changed: Incentives are now recognized as a policy instrument; a search is being made for an incentive system which would produce the results desired by the national leadership.

The shift away from directive planning toward incentive planning was accompanied in all the soviet-type economies by the relegation of certain powers to lower administrative levels. In some countries, as in the Soviet Union, administration was regionalized. In Poland, regional bodies play a minor role, but some ministerial powers were given to consortia set up to supervise groups of enterprises working in the same branch of industry.

Decentralization frees the national authorities from the task of making a large number of minute decisions. In Poland, for instance, some 2,500 products were centrally allocated before the reforms; the current list of centrally al-

---

his assertions on figures quoted from the *Socialisticheskii trud,* no. 4, 1959.

[24] Speech of W. Gomułka at the 3d Congress of the PZPR, *op. cit.,* p. 91.

located products contains only approximately 250 items. As was already mentioned, before 1956 the national plan specified in detail 80 per cent of the assortments. The current plans specify 55 per cent of the assortments and indicate the remaining 45 per cent in aggregates, leaving detailed decisions to lower levels. As a consequence, the communication channels are less strained. The central authorities are free to concentrate on major decisions, and their control over general policy is strengthened.

Administrative decentralization does not necessarily increase reliance on indirect inducements, nor does it necessarily increase the freedom of operating units to make their own decisions. Eighty-eight per cent of Polish enterprises report that the transfer of policy powers from ministries to consortia does not increase their freedom of action.[25] The consortium or the regional body is better able to keep in touch with the operating level than is the national administration; yet the bureaucrats' desire for power may effectively prevent enterprises from influencing policy.

The flexibility of the system and the autonomy of enterprises were increased not so much by the administrative reforms as by the reduction in the number of directives, carried out at the same time. The changes which took place since 1956 are best illustrated by the example of cost directives.

Some fifteen separate directives were issued to every Polish enterprise before the 1956 reforms; three of them dealt specifically with production costs. Of these, one indicated the permissible cost of production, another the ratio

[25] Rada Ekonomiczna przy Radzie Ministrów, *Sytuacja gospodarcza kraju w roku 1959*, pp. 41–42.

of costs of material inputs to total costs, and a third one showed planned cost reductions. The cost-reduction index does not seem to have had a notable influence on production costs. "In the year 1953 alone—we are told—the economic loss attributable to the failure to fulfill the cost-reduction plan amounted to 1.2 billion złotys." [26]

Even when the cost directives were followed, the effect was highly conjectural. Since the input prices were fixed in an arbitrary fashion, the cost directives could be followed by appropriate assortment manipulations. As prices were changed, all cost indices had to be recalculated—a complex and time-consuming job. Indeed, it was never quite clear whether the reported costs corresponded to real cost changes, or whether they reflected price changes and assortment manipulations. [27]

Reforms swept away all the cost directives and replaced them with an incentive to achieve cost reductions. Under the new system, each enterprise has a fund which can be used for specified purposes, including bonus payments, company housing, and the provision of cultural and recreational facilities. The fund is fed with a portion of the planned profit achieved by each enterprise. If a greater profit than planned is achieved, the fund is correspondingly increased.

Enterprise funds provide a highly flexible policy tool. If policy makers wish to concentrate on cost decreases, they may increase the scale of bonuses for profit achievement.

[26] Bolesław Bierut's speech at the 2d Congress of the PZPR, see *II Zjazd PZPR; Sprawozdanie KC PZPR*, Warszawa, Książka i Wiedza, 1954, p. 56.

[27] Stefan Hatt, "O właściwej roli planowania obniżki kosztów własnych," *Gospodarka Planowa*, vol. 15, no. 8, 1960.

To bring to light hidden production capacities, enterprises may be permitted to put into their fund part of the monies obtained from the sale of superfluous equipment and machinery. Fund uses are also readily subject to regulation. If wage payments are excessive, enterprises may be directed to use their funds for housing or social purposes and cut back on bonuses. Conversely, when there are too many housing starts, the construction of company housing may be blocked. Thus the creation of an over-all financial incentive eliminates the need for specific cost directives, without any abdication of the administration's powers.

Financial incentives are part of a broader incentive scheme now in force. The main incentives are still concerned with physical output achievement, but financial considerations play an increasing role.

Under the new system of incentives introduced in Poland in 1960, the premium funds are divided into basic funds and supplementary funds. The basic premiums are equal to 10 to 30 per cent of the white-collar workers' base pay. The premiums paid for matching the previous year's (physical and financial) performance are scaled down if the performance level is not reached. The head of the enterprise obtains the premium automatically, while premiums paid to other white-collar workers are at the discretion of the top management. Supplementary premiums paid for the improvement of plan results are received only by heads of enterprises and departments. The highest bonus (15 to 20 per cent of base pay) is paid when a large improvement is planned and the plan is exactly achieved. The bonus is smaller if a less taut plan is overfulfilled or a more ambitious plan is underfulfilled. As a consequence, the new scheme gives an incentive toward taut but feasible planning.

Supplementary premiums are contingent upon the fulfillment of several conditions. No premiums can be paid unless the physical production plan is met and the enterprise keeps wage payments within the wage fund limits. In the machine-tool industry, premiums are not paid if delivery delays occur. Additional conditions (such as assortment specifications) may be imposed on enterprises by the respective trusts. All conditions may be waived at the discretion of the ministry in charge of the given branch of the economy.[28]

Bonuses for physical and financial performance are supposed to reward effort and are not conceived as a measure of absolute performance. In order to make the tasks facing individual enterprises more equal, Polish consortia received permission in 1960 to treat each of its subordinate enterprises on an individual basis, within limits determined by the respective ministry. The consortia were instructed to set up rewards proportional to the magnitude of tasks assigned to individual enterprises and to the difficulty of achieving further improvement. An enterprise which is already well managed should therefore be rewarded more amply than one which is not, and similarly, an enterprise which has a very taut plan should receive more of a premium for overfulfillment than one with an easy task.[29]

In practice, differentiation among enterprises leads to

[28] Bronisław Fick, "Nowy system płac pracowników umysłowych w przemyśle," *Finanse,* vol. 11, no. 2, pp. 24–30, 1960.

[29] Directive issued on Dec. 31, 1959, *Dziennik Ustaw,* no. 4, January 24, 1960, position 24, paragraph 7, point 2, and Resolution of the Council of Ministers, no. 24, January 25, 1960.

insurmountable difficulties. Since efforts are initially made to set up goals of equal difficulty for all enterprises, a second round of goal appraisal merely shows up mistakes in the initial plans. Moreover, differential treatment is likely to lead to accusations of discrimination and favoritism. As a consequence, trusts tend to take the easiest way out and draw up identical incentive schemes for all the enterprises.[30]

Delays and the delivery of defective goods provoked legislation (introduced during the Stalinist era, but reinforced since) to levy penalties on the delinquent enterprises. When a product is too defective to serve its original purpose, it is reclassified and receives lesser weight in the computation of goal fulfillment. Moreover, delinquent enterprises must pay fines to the enterprises which suffer a loss through either nondelivery or delivery of defective materials.[31] The system provides a quality incentive, but it is not foolproof. As long as the inputs are delivered, it is simpler to utilize them regardless of their defectiveness, as long as the output is also sold, rather than return the goods and await redress. The fines are fixed at conventional levels, and they do not always correspond to the extent of the loss; they also lead to endless litigations to fix the blame on the guilty party.

Partisans of incentive planning had great expectations that the curtailment of directives and an increased reliance

[30] See Marek Misiak, "Bodźce napiętego planowania?" *Życie Gospodarcze* no. 1, 1961. See also the same author's "Sprzeczności bodźców," *ibid.*, no. 12, 1961.

[31] See *Dziennik Ustaw Rrzeczpospolitej Polskiej*, 11.24.1950, no. 53, position 503 and *Monitor Polski*, 11.2.1956, no. 98, position 1016.

on incentives would bring a marked improvement in the efficiency of the economy. Though no one would deny that some improvement took place, the hopes were largely disappointed. The curtailment of directives ". . . led to the weakening of some controls which are essential for the regulation of economic activity by the state. New, equally effective methods of control were not developed in their stead." [32]

The operation of a planning scheme through incentives is infinitely more complex than directive planning. A directive states explicitly the response which the authorities desire to obtain. In an incentive scheme the degree of response is always a matter of conjecture. If expectations are not realized, the incentive has to be changed.

Situations in which an incentive scheme can elicit only one type of response are extremely rare. In general, to each incentive there correspond a number of possible actions. The Stalinist physical plan overfulfillment bonus was meant to provide a production incentive, but in fact the bonus also provided incentives toward the concealment of production potential and toward assortment shifts. The current Polish incentive schemes attempt to eliminate the undesirable modes of action by weighing the various actions in the computation of a bonus. In computing managerial bonuses, planned increases, plan achievement, cost reductions, and quality changes are weighed to yield a global result. The weights of the bonus system are in effect prices on which

[32] Stefan Jędrychowski, "Niektóre problemy ulepszania gospodarki narodowej" (lecture delivered at a conference of Party activists of the Central Planning Commission), *Gospodarka Planowa*, vol. 14, no. 2, p. 1, 1960.

management bases its actions to maximize managerial income.

As the complexity of the inducement schemes increases, it is increasingly difficult to determine the effect which each inducement price will have. The incentive for cost minimization was included in the Polish scheme to lower production costs and save on scarce inputs. Yet, where the factory prices of inputs were not fixed correctly, the effects were contrary to those intended. This was the case in steel utilization. Though steel was in high demand, its factory price was fixed in Poland at a low level. As a consequence, despite the cost-reduction incentive, steel is said to be used 20 to 30 per cent less efficiently in Poland than in the Soviet Union and Western Europe.[33] Rather than try to change the price of steel or to give greater bonuses for steel saving, the Polish council of ministers decreed that the machine-tool industry must save 4 per cent of steel per machine per year in the period from 1961 to 1965 relative to the initial plan estimates. Even greater economies were decreed for the construction industry, especially for residential construction.[34]

The greatest disappointment to the advocates of incentive planning was caused by the failure of the Polish decentralized investment scheme. Under the scheme, enterprises were permitted to utilize part of their enterprise funds for invest-

[33] Adam Stupnicki, "Zagadnienie oszczędności stali," *Inwestycje i Budownictwo,* vol. 11, no. 2, 1961.

[34] *Ibid.* The drive to save steel is criticized, however, because it results in an excessive use of wood (especially in construction). The obvious conclusion is that wood, too, is underpriced. See Wiesław Głowacki, "Kosztowna sprzeczność," *Życie Gospodarcze,* no. 15, 1961.

ment purposes. If the investments were productive, they would increase physical output possibilities and/or decrease production costs, thus raising the pay of both workers and management. Since the decentralized investments were financed by the enterprise's own funds and the enterprise itself was to decide on the nature of investment, there was a stronger incentive for efficient resource use than in the case of planned investments financed by budgetary allotment.

In practice, it soon became apparent that decentralized investments competed for producer goods with the centrally planned investments. The volume and character of decentralized investments could not be predicted with great accuracy, and controls were gradually reintroduced. In the end, nothing remained of the decentralized investments except the name and the formal difference in the source of finance. All investment projects, except for trifling improvements, must now receive ministerial approval and must be incorporated in the over-all plan.

The multiplicity of pricing schemes prevailing in the soviet-type economies greatly complicates the task of planning through incentives. In free-enterprise economies, the major incentive is the profit motive, but that incentive operates within a uniform price scheme. Every enterprise faces a choice of actions, such as changes in the volume of production, assortment, or production technique. The profitability of each type of action provides a uniform priority list. There is no uniform priority list in the soviet-type economies. Consequently, the reliance on financial incentives has inherent limitations:

To interest an enterprise to the largest possible extent in lowering production costs, it is necessary to limit the possibility of increasing profits through changes in assortment. As a consequence the influence of price differentials on assortment must be decreased.[35]

A problem of this type cannot arise in a single-price system in which changes in assortment and input mix are measured by a common monetary denominator. In a soviet-type economy the policy makers want to influence the product mix independently of the choice of inputs. The use of financial incentives to reduce costs runs afoul of the desire to set outputs regardless of output profitability and requires the imposition of a stricter control on the product mix.

The leadership in the soviet-type economies is reluctant and (one might suspect) incapable of administering a planning system which would rely primarily on price manipulation. The administrative tasks of such a system would be formidable. During the 1961 Polish price reform, the prices of 12,000 chemical products had to be changed. The complete price list of the Polish chemical industry contains 250,000 items and the price list of the mechanical industry 100,000 items. The computations and the forms required for the change of the factory price of an agricultural machine composed of 50 separate parts require under the current procedure the use of 1,500 sheets of paper[36] and an un-

[35] Z. Fedorowicz, "Finanse w gospodarce socjalistycznej," Warszawa, Polskie Wydawnictwa Gospodarcze, 1960, p. 23.

[36] Władysław Dudziński, "Ceny fabryczne," *Życie Gospodarcze,* no. 15, 1961.

specified number of man-hours. Little wonder that the frequency of price adjustments is kept to a minimum.

Changes in product prices affect the production costs of all the enterprises using the products as inputs. If prices were to be used as a current policy tool, the entire price system would have to be constantly recalculated. Such constant recalculations are impracticable, and the adjustments are not made. As a consequence, prices tend to be detached from the economic relations, regardless of the theoretical foundations of the price system. This detachment of prices from scarcity relations acts in turn as a bar to the use of prices as a primary policy tool.

Theoretical objections to the use of prices as a policy instrument are succinctly summarized by Prof. Bronisław Minc, one of the more orthodox Polish Marxists:

> The "signals" transmitted through price-profit changes are as a rule out of date, since they show the result of changes which have taken place in the past . . . [moreover] they do not lead to a quantitative appraisal of necessary changes. For instance, a 50 per cent increase in the price of a product does not mean that there is need for a 50 per cent increase in quantity of that product.

As a consequence when one relies on the price-profit mechanism,

> It is impossible to make coordinated decisions concerning the entire economy; one can only arrive at uncoordinated partial decisions which will be undertaken with a greater or less delay.[37]

[37] Bronisław Minc, "Cel gospodarki, planowanie i produkcja towarowa w socjalizmie," *Gospodarka Planowa*, vol. 15, no. 4, 1960, p. 20.

Many economists in Poland and other countries of the Soviet camp would take exception to the theoretical underpinnings of Professor Minc's statements. There is little doubt, however, that Minc's diagnosis of the policy makers' dislike of price policy is essentially correct. Two cases will illustrate the point. In both cases there was choice between direct action and price changes. In both of them direct action was preferred, much for the reasons outlined by Minc.

In 1959, when decentralized investments still played a major role, the accumulation of investment funds surpassed the availability of investment goods at the existing price level:

The situation could have been solved either through an increase in the price of investment goods, or by blocking certain investment funds. The latter solution, which was adopted in 1959, appears to be preferable. An increase in the price of investment goods guarantees that equilibrium will be restored, but it does not give the assurance that the remaining investment funds will be used in the best manner from the point of view of the national economy.[38]

Since prices are largely detached from scarcity relations, profits are not necessarily a good indicator of urgency of need. Planned investments have a higher national priority than decentralized investments; thus, if some investments are to be curtailed, direct action is preferable to elimination through price changes.

The second case illustrates more convincingly the diffi-

[38] Eugeniusz Rychlewski, "O dwuch pułapach i stopie wzrostu inwestycji w roku 1959," *Gospodarka Planowa*, vol. 15, no. 5, p. 7, 1960.

culties of controlling side effects of allocation policies which
rely on administrative price changes. In the middle 1950s,
rising workers' wages and meat price controls resulted in an
acute meat shortage. To eliminate the shortage, meat prices
were increased by 25 per cent in 1959. The increase in meat
prices caused a decline in demand for consumer durables,
from which one can deduce that demand for meat has a
low price elasticity. As a result of the decline in demand,
consumer durables inventories accumulated. Here the price
setters found themselves in a dilemma. One suggested course
of action would be an increase in money wages paid to
workers. The price setters felt, however, that income elasticity of demand for food is so high that increased money
wages would necessitate increases in food prices. There
would have been a transfer of real income from workers to
farmers, and such a transfer is deemed socially undesirable.
Decreases in consumer durable prices were opposed because price setters believe that demand for such goods is
highly inelastic. Thus lower prices would lead to an excess
of purchasing power which would be spent on food.[39]

Whether or not the planners' estimates of price elastic-
ities are correct, the experience illustrates the general problem of price manipulation in a planned economy. Any price
change has repercussions on demand for other goods (unless, perchance, demand elasticity is unity). One price
change leads to the necessity of adjusting other prices. In
the process there are distributive effects which policy
makers oppose. To avoid such effects the simplest course
is one of isolating the difficulties through direct allocation.
Since price changes have repercussions which cannot always be foreseen and might be unfavorable, the best policy

[39] *Ibid.*

is to leave prices alone and take direct action. Once more we must agree with Professor Minc that despite all the recent reforms, ". . . the reliance on physical entities in planning and in choosing among alternatives is a characteristic trait of socialist economies. Financial tasks are treated as derived tasks and not as independent entities." [40] Price manipulation and the use of quasi-price incentives have their place within the system, but the core is direct, nonprice allocation and goal-setting through directives.

The relegation of financial planning and price policy to a subordinate role raises serious problems of control over the economy. Since prices are administratively fixed, price movements cannot be used as indicators of economic performance. Moreover, since prices are arbitrarily fixed and there is a multiplicity of implicit and explicit price systems, enterprise financial reports are at best a vague reflection of performance:

> If an enterprise shows revenues which are lower than the planned revenues, we may conclude that it did not meet its production goals. The enterprise might not be able to meet its goals for a variety of reasons: The volume of production might have fallen off, the assortment might have been changed, the quality of production might have declined, or, finally, the customers might not have met their financial obligations. The signal [i.e., the inability to meet financial goals] is therefore ambiguous. [41]

If the leadership wishes to manipulate separately the volume of production, the assortment, and the costs of

[40] Bronisław Minc, "Cel gospodarki, planowanie i produkcja towarowa w socjalizmie," *op. cit.*, p. 20.
[41] Z. Fedorowicz, *op. cit.*, p. 79.

production, a global figure showing profit or loss is of little
help toward decision making.

c. Inventories as a Signaling Device

Where prices are rigid and the meaning of financial statements uncertain, inventory control might seem to provide
a promising "feedback" device:

> In an economy directed by a plan, in which prices do not
> vary freely in response to market conditions, the structure and
> nature of inventories held by enterprises provides the best
> "barometer" signaling economic disequilibria.[42]

A rise in inventories could be taken as an indication of
excessive output and a fall as an indication of impending
shortage. Quick administrative action based on up-to-date
inventory reports could maintain market balance even in
the absence of flexible prices.

The practical problems of reliance on inventory data for
information feedback are very grave. Inventories are ascertained in periodic audits, and the reports reach policy makers
with considerable delay. Even if it were possible to compute
inventories on a continuous basis (which would be no mean
feat in itself), the question of interpretation of inventory
movements would remain to be solved.

Inventories are held to ensure the periodicity of production in the face of uneven input flows and of uneven demand
for output. Inventories are also held in anticipation of con-

[42] P. Sulmicki, "Zapasy i kredyt obrotowy," *Narodowy Bank
Polski, Wiadomości*, vol. 14, no. 3, 1958.

tingencies, such as machinery breakdowns. A rise in inventories might occur in anticipation of a production speedup, as a consequence of change in production technique or the nature of the product. None of the changes in any way reflects changes in the supply and demand equilibrium.

The signals relevant to the policy maker consist of involuntary changes in inventory levels. Inventories rise when the produce finds no outlet, and they fall when there is a shortage. Unfortunately it is impossible to distinguish between the voluntary and involuntary changes without an extremely detailed investigation which could not be made on a continuous basis.

To stem the accumulation of inventories, the permissible inventory level is prescribed in terms of financial norms. The definition of the optimal inventory level is a complex technical problem, especially in a system in which physical allocation plays a prime role and prices are detached from scarcity relations. As a consequence, norms ". . . tend to be determined by the financial possibilities of the state budget rather than by the economically justifiable needs of the enterprises." [43]

Conformity with inventory norms is enforced through the banking system. When an enterprise surpasses its normal working capital needs, it must obtain additional credit. In 1957, the emergency credit bore a penal 18 per cent interest rate. In subsequent years the rate was lowered, but the use of the penal interest rates was more strictly enforced. These measures had one unforeseen effect: The mutual indebtedness of enterprises assumed the role of near-money. Overdue accounts payable amounted to 11 per cent of all accounts

[43] L. Gluck, *op. cit.*, p. 62.

payable at the end of 1957, and to 37 per cent of all accounts payable at the end of 1959.[44]

Attempts to enforce the inventory norms met with something less than total success, judging by a comparison of planned inventory changes with actual inventory changes (see Table 8).

Table 8   Planned and actual inventory increases in Poland, 1953 to 1958 (in billions of złotys)

Year	Planned	Actual
1953	12.6	18.9
1954	8.1	9.9
1955	4.9	11.1
1956	4.1	7.8
1957	7.7	21.8
1958	11.2	21.1

Source: L. Gluck, "Zagadnienie zapasów w gospodarce narodowej," *Narodowy Bank Polski, Wiadomości,* vol. 15, no. 2, 1959, p. 61.

Over the period from 1953 to 1958, increases in inventories amounted on the average to 5.1 per cent of the increase in national income. In the OEEC countries, by contrast, inventory increases amount to 1.5 per cent of income increases on the average.[45]

[44] W. Jaworski, "Rola banku w likwidacji przyczyn wzajemnego zadłużania się przedsiębiorstw," *Narodowy Bank Polski, Wiadomości,* vol. 15, no. 11, pp. 542ff., 1959.

[45] L. Gluck, *op. cit.,* p. 61. Note that the figures for Poland and for the OECC countries are not strictly comparable because of the peculiarities of the Polish price system and because of differences in the method of national income calculation.

Statistical reports which differentiate between various categories of inventories are exceedingly unreliable. Enterprises have a strong incentive to under-report inventories of faulty or unusable goods, for such goods cannot be covered by inventory norms. Even so, the reported unsalable inventories amounted to 4.4 billion złotys as of June 1, 1958, that is, to some 5 per cent of total new investment in that year.[46]

Hand in hand with the excessive accumulation of inventories goes a perennial inventory shortage. The two phenomena are not unconnected. Even if an over-all inventory balance were attained, excessive inventory holdings by one firm result in inventory shortages for another. By hoarding inventories each firm ensures a better periodicity of its own production, at the cost of production periodicity of other firms. The situation is further aggravated by mistakes in assortment which create over-all shortages of certain goods.

The simplest solution to the inventory problem is also the least acceptable to the system. If every enterprise had an incentive to keep inventories at a level which maximizes the return on the enterprise investment, excess inventories would melt away. Inventories could then conceivably be used as a signalling device.

The difficulties of keeping inventories at an economically justifiable level are readily traced to the subordination of financial goals to physical output goals. If every enterprise aimed at profit maximization, it would attempt to keep inventories on a profit-maximizing level. Under the current system, the larger the inventory the better, since output maximization is the primary goal. When mistakes in input

[46] *Ibid.*, p. 63.

planning or in output production occur, they also add to the inventory total and further obscure the picture.

Deprived of meaningful financial data, meaningful price data, and meaningful inventory figures, the policy makers in soviet-type economies must muddle through by piecing together physical and financial performance information. With little precise knowledge and with only a vague idea of the interconnections within the economy, it is perhaps best to continue to rely on directives, rather than to use incentives and face unforeseeable consequences which may be more difficult to cope with than the original problem.

7

Efficiency and Waste

The efficiency of an economy must be judged in terms of the system's aims. Partisans of the free market are willing to put up with some economic waste in order to preserve certain social and political freedoms, and partisans of soviet-type economies are willing to make similar sacrifices for their own ideals.

What one system defines as a valuable product, another may look upon as waste. To a Soviet critic the product variation and advertising which occur in capitalist countries are examples of waste, yet the capitalist countries include such "waste" in their national product calculations.[1] The

[1] Not a few Western economists deplore the waste of resources in free enterprise countries on "unnecessary" products. Thus Hansen:

A not inconsiderable part of our productive resources is wasted on artificially created wants. Machines with 300 horsepower, weighing two tons or more, are standard utility conveyance

forced development of heavy industry which occurs in Soviet nations is wasteful by free-market standards, yet it is one of the fundamental goals of the Soviet systems.

The achievements or shortcomings of an economy are best judged in terms of the problems which the economy is able (or unable) to solve. The temptation is great to compare the actual performance of the soviet-type system with an idealized free-market economy. To avoid such a temptation I shall endeavor to distinguish difficulties which arise through the imperfect application of a sound principle from the difficulties inherent in the system itself.

The soviet-type system is capable of coping with the unemployment problem. There is always sufficient effective demand to absorb all the goods produced. Hence, there is effective demand for all the available labor.

The demand for goods and services, and indirectly the demand for labor, is generated by governmental action. The demand for consumer goods is regulated by the authorities through the adjustment of retail prices in relation to wage payments. When consumer goods are in excess supply,

---

for one single person—the typical scene on any American highway. Involved is not only waste of materials and productive man power, but also the waste of a highly essential and limited energy resource. This is only one example of the waste we see all about us in this rich country of ours. (Alvin G. Hansen, *Economic Issues of the 1960's*, New York, McGraw-Hill Book Company, Inc., 1960, pp. 46–47.)

The distinction between an "artificially created want" and a "natural" one is clearly one of ethical and moral judgment, since virtually all our wants are "created" by our environment. Ultimately our appraisal of "waste" rests on a subjective appraisal of value, since there is no empirical way to determine what people "ought" to have.

retail prices are lowered or wages are raised until the excess is taken off the market. The demand for producer goods is generated directly by the national investment plans. Since most investments are made through budgetary allotment, the recipient enterprises and regional authorities exert a constant pressure for more investment.

The system is propelled forward by rewards for high-volume production. The more produced, the higher the rewards of labor and management. The enterprise has little concern with the profitability of its operations; its aim is the maximization of output. Thus, enterprises will tend to hire all the workers who make any positive contribution to the product, regardless of the cost of labor and the value of the marginal product.

Full employment is achieved at the cost of some labor resource misallocation. Since wages are administratively set and are not related to the value of the workers' product, there is little incentive to limit employment in individual industries to the economically justified level. There is also no automatic mechanism for enticing workers to branches of industry in which they are most urgently needed.

If in enterprise X there arises a surplus of 100 workers, these workers could be shifted to other new or expanding enterprises. There is, however, no mechanism which would induce the shifting of those workers to other branches of the economy. As a consequence a surplus of labor remains in the given enterprise.[2]

The wastage of human resources which results from a soviet-type labor mobilization policy must be compared with the wastage under alternate solutions. A perfectly competi-

[2] Mieczysław Kabaj, "Mechanizm zatrudnienia w gospodarce socjalistycznej," *Ekonomista*, no. 1, p. 61, 1960.

tive, frictionless economy with no price rigidities might result—in theory—in full employment and efficient labor use. None of the existing free-market economies approaches this ideal. In prewar Poland, Czechoslovakia, Rumania, or Hungary—to name only four countries in which soviet-type regimes have been established since the war—the labor market was highly imperfect, as was the capital and the product market. There was perennial unemployment, and even the employed workers were poorly allocated—witness the substantial superiority of industrial over agricultural wages. If the prewar labor allocation is compared with the allocation in the Soviet-bloc countries in the postwar period, there is little doubt that labor resources are more fully utilized in the latter period.

The ability of the leadership to mobilize human resources and its discretionary power in determining the pattern of production explain the remarkably high rates of growth achieved by the soviet-type economies. In the free-enterprise countries, the market dictates to a large extent the proportion of resources which will be allocated to future uses. In the soviet-type economies, the leadership determines the rate of investment, subject only to over-all political and social considerations. Investment can be concentrated in industries which build a base for further investment. Instead of investing in automobile body dyes, one can invest in the manufacturing of machine tools which will be used to make more machine tools.

By free-enterprise standards the growth policy of the soviet-type economies is not rational. If the market were permitted to function, the production pattern would be dictated by market considerations. In so far as the allocation dictated by the Soviet policy makers deviates from the market pattern, it is irrational in market terms. Demonstrating that the soviet-type systems grow faster does not prove their superiority any more than demonstrating that free-enterprise countries produce more consumer goods proves the reverse.

We may legitimately inquire whether the soviet-type system of allocation results in an efficient investment pattern in terms of its own value scheme. Even this question could not have been raised as long as the theory of the all-knowing state prevailed. At the height of the Stalinist period, Prof. Bronisław Minc gave a terse description of the investment process:

> The choice of investments is determined by the economic and political tasks placed in front of society in the given stage of its development by the government and the party of the working class.[3]

As long as one assumes that the leadership is all-knowing, and as long as the leadership decides on all details of investments, there can be no question of rationality. The tasks are assigned at will. If they are faithfully carried out, the leadership's wishes are satisfied and investment, in the leadership's terms, is rational.

The acceptance of the leadership's infallibility suggests plan fulfillment figures as a method of efficiency measurement. Unfortunately, the fulfillment figures are very ambiguous. When annual plans are issued with a substantial delay, they report in part on past accomplishments instead of

[3] Bronisław Minc, "O efektywności inwestycji w gospodarce socjalistyznej," *Ekonomista*, January, 1951.

mapping out future production. Moreover, plans can be ful-
filled or overfulfilled by appropriate manipulation of the
product mix. For instance, in 1958, 243 investment projects
were scheduled for completion in Poland, but only 116 were
completed. Yet, "in accordance with the value indices applied as a gauge of project fulfillment, the 1958 plan was
deemed overfulfilled," and appropriate premiums were
paid.[4]

When fulfillment figures depart too radically from the
plan figures, the plan may be amended to reflect expected
performance. The 1959 Polish investment plan foresaw centralized investments valued at 44.7 billion złotys. In the
course of the planned year investments valued at 600 million
złotys were deleted, but other investments were increased
by 2.5 million złotys to reflect changes in cost estimates.
Actual investments for the year amounted to 45.8 billion,
which is lower than the final figure but higher than the
initial plan.[5]

If one abandons the doctrine of the infallibility of the
leadership, plan fulfillment no longer can be considered as
an objective basis for efficiency judgment. Plans which are
overambitious or inconsistent can be overfulfilled, while
plans which underestimate productive capacity can be surpassed. Even Bronisław Minc in his more recent writings
admits that the leadership must tailor its demands to reality,
and that the tailoring does not always fit. According to
Minc, the investment planning process should start with a
political decision concerning the global volume of invest-

[4] Rada Ekonomiczna przy Radzie Ministrów, *Sytuacja
gospodarcza kraju w roku 1959*, p. 98, footnote 1.
[5] *Ibid.*, pp. 106–108.

ment and the major investment objects. The decision may be modified in view of input availability; e.g., the construction industry may not have the capacity to undertake the planned construction or the steel industry may not have the steel-making capacity to produce the planned machine tools. The final plan must also take into account the equilibrium of the consumer goods market, since investments generate wages without increasing the output of consumer goods.[6]

Actual planning practice goes much further in the direction of weighing of alternatives. Political considerations continue to play a dominant role, but the question of economic rationality of the political decisions is raised with increasing frequency. In Poland, which is in the forefront of economic reforms in the socialist camp, economic calculus played a modest role as early as 1955:

As is well known, the Six-Year Plan was prepared primarily on the material balancing technique. Economic calculations, such as we understand them now, played only a minimal role. In the final stages of preparation of the 1955–1960 Six-Year Plan many economic analyses of investment efficiency were carried out. Some of these were taken into account in the final version of the plan. The methodology of economic calculus has not been introduced in a permanent fashion into planning, however.[7]

In the preparation of the current (1961 to 1965) plan, the volume of calculations and the importance attached to them

[6] Bronisław Minc, "Problemy teorii inwestowania w gospodarce socjalistycznej," *Ekonomista*, no. 3, pp. 460–476, 1960.

[7] Witold Lissowski, "Problemy określania właściwego poziomu i kierunków inwestycji produkcyjnych w planie perspektywicznym," *Gospodarka Planowa*, vol. 13, no. 2, 1958, p. 17.

increased markedly. The same trend is evident in all the nations of the Soviet camp.

The admission that economic calculations are useful is tantamount to the acceptance of an outside standard of efficiency measurement. The need for calculations and the possibility of applying an outside standard increase as planning becomes less specific. When the growth of every industry and the method by which the growth is to be achieved are politically determined, there is no possibility of choice among alternatives, hence no possibility of a calculus. If the policy goals are expressed in broad aggregates, one can consider alternate methods of reaching the goals.

During the Stalinist period, economic calculations were confined to comparisons between alternate methods of manufacturing a given product. Even such calculations were severely handicapped by doctrinal considerations. Marxist theory does not include interest on capital or rent in the calculation of economic costs, though depreciation is taken into account. As a consequence, cost calculations are reduced to comparisons of current input costs. When a technique requiring heavy initial investment with small current inputs is compared with one in which the initial investment is small but current inputs are higher, the former technique is favored under the Marxist scheme.

In comparing the effectiveness of a thermal plant with a hydroelectric plant, to take an example, the amount of resources tied up in capital construction is not taken into account. Since the thermal plant depreciates faster and requires more current inputs than a hydroelectric plant, the latter seems more effective when the Marxist concept of cost is applied.

Since the middle 1950s, the ban on interest on capital has been removed. The Polish Planning Commission, for example, imputes a 12 per cent interest on capital when making investment effectiveness calculations. This rate was picked by a trial and error method: a higher rate rejected too many projects, while at a lower rate more projects were profitable than could be accommodated within the investment plan. A few words of explanation are needed here to clarify the meaning of an interest rate which is "too high" or "too low" in a direct allocation situation.

The rationing of investment funds and the direct allocation of certain inputs does not preclude the possibility of performing economic calculations within individual branches of the economy. Investment projects may be ranked from most profitable to least profitable in terms of the factor prices, and "shadow prices" may be assigned to the factors which are directly allocated. The implicit interest rate is such a shadow price. If the rate is picked correctly, it equates the demand for investment in the individual branch of industry with the amount of funds allocated to that branch.

While formal calculations are rarely if ever performed, the technicians who draw up investment projects have an approximate idea of the interest rate implicit in their branch of the economy. The rate is often expressed in terms of payout periods rather than interest, but the basic concepts are the same. The 12 per cent rate picked by the Polish Planning Commission represents a rough average of the implicit rates prevailing in the economy.

To formalize the method of investment effectiveness calculations, the Polish Planning Commission issues detailed methodological instructions. With the progress of the Commission's labors, these instructions become progressively more intricate, and by now they surpass the economic administrators' ability to calculate.[8]

To perform calculations of investment effectiveness it does not suffice to have a method; it is also necessary to have an incentive to calculate. In the soviet-type system the incentive is very weak, since very little depends on the correctness of the results. The acceptance of investment projects depends largely on the strategy of presentation. Once the project is accepted and the investment is carried out, the economic effectiveness is of little concern to the management entrusted with the operation of the new enterprise. The rewards to management are given for plan fulfillment and improving performance, not for the absolute results.

A measure of efficiency of plants built under the Communist regime may be obtained by comparing the current production costs of such plants with the production costs of older plants built under free enterprise in the same country. A comparison of production costs (exclusive of capital charges) of plants built in Poland during the Six-Year Plan (1949 to 1955) with those of plants built before 1939 shows that the latter are in most cases more efficient.

[8] See Komisja Planowania przy Radzie Ministrów, *Instrukcja ogólna w sprawie metodyki badań ekonomicznej efektywności inwestycji*, Warszawa, 1960. This set of instructions is over 40 pages long and contains many intricate formulas. I discussed its use with the managerial personnel of several enterprises, who assured me that they continued to rely on accepted engineers' rules of thumb, while pretending to follow the letter of the instructions which to them were quite incomprehensible.

Efficiency and Waste   **227**

From Table 9 it is evident that in terms of current costs
the new establishments have a distinct current cost advantage in the field of electric energy generation only, whereas
in the other industries current costs of new establishments
are equal if not higher than the costs of old firms, many of
which have been in operation for twenty years or more.

Table 9 *Cost of production in new plants*
as percentage of average cost of
all plants in the industry (as of
1957)

Iron and steel industry	90–105
Electric energy	61–81
Chemical industry	100–139
Construction materials	107–138
Paper manufacturing	108 *
Textile industry	91–101
Breweries	112–114

* One new paper mill only.
Source: Z. Sprycha, "Czy pesymistyczne głosy o kosztach w nowych
zakładach są uzasadnione?" *Gospodarka Planowa*, vol. 13, no. 4, pp. 5ff.,
1958.

The above comparisons are biased in favor of the new establishments, since costs are computed on the basis of 1957
prices, while the prewar establishments were adapted to the
then-prevailing price levels. Moreover, in prewar years
private enterprise had to reckon with the cost of capital,
whereas capital outlays were not calculated in the Six-Year-
Plan investments. Thus the older establishments may have
deliberately used a higher ratio of current outlays compared
with capital outlays than the new ones. The inclusion of
a realistic allowance for capital charges would turn the com-

parison even more in favor of older plants. To counter-
weigh this bias, one has to take into account the "teething
troubles" of many new firms. Indeed, year-to-year comparisons show an improvement in the new firms' performance
relative to the average. Yet even when this improvement
is reckoned, the resulting picture shows a net regression
rather than progress.

Even if investment effectiveness calculations were con-
scientiously performed in each branch of industry, the effectiveness of investment would not be maximized for the
economy as a whole as long as capital is rationed. Some
branches of industry are favored by the political leadership,
and investment funds are amply provided although the effectiveness of the investment is low. In other branches a
high cutoff rate must be applied. The political considerations
governing the differential efficiency standards are readily
admitted by the leadership:

It is necessary to maintain our policy of a high rate of accumulation [i.e., of a high profit margin] in the textile industry
for two reasons. First, the textile industry relies to a great extent on imported raw materials. Second, it is necessary to maintain the high rate of accumulation, because of the need to maintain a low rate of accumulation in other branches of industry.[9]

Unprofitable investments must be made in some branches
of industry favored by the leadership. To finance these investments, large profits must be extracted in other branches.

In laying out development plans, the political leadership

[9] Władysław Gomułka, "Wprowadzenie do dyskusji nad
referatem Biura Politycznego," *V Plenum KC PZPR*, Warszawa,
Książka i Wiedza, 1960, p. 22.

frequently contrasts "national interest" (i.e., political choice) with investment efficiency:

> There is a sharp contrast between the effectiveness of investment in the two branches of production [between the machine tool industry and coal mining]. Reckoned in 1956 prices, machine tool production increased between 1949 and 1959 by a factor of almost seven and a half. In spite of greater investment the output of coal mining rose by only 66.5 per cent in the like period. . . . Nevertheless, we must increase our investment in the extractive industry, which provides the raw material base for our entire industry.[10]

In principle, any investment which ranks high on a national priority list should be highly effective in terms of the same list. The discrepancy arises because there is no correspondence between the scarcity relations prevailing in the economy and the prices used for investment efficiency calculations.

Investment efficiency calculations are normally performed on the basis of factory prices; these in turn are based on production costs plus a conventional profit margin. The cost computations leave much to be desired. For example, even though the planning office now uses an interest rate in ranking investment projects, interest is not imputed in the enterprise cost calculations. As a consequence, the cost of production of capital-intensive goods is underestimated relative to the cost of production of labor-intensive goods.

Factory prices are set in most Soviet-bloc countries on the average cost level of every branch of industry. This practice was criticized by many Polish economists. During the de-

[10] *Ibid.*, pp. 19–20.

bate of the 1950s, strong pleas were heard for marginal cost pricing or at least for pricing on the level of the average cost of the marginal enterprise in each industry.[11]

The critics did not perceive that costs, whether marginal or average, cannot be determined until the production decision is reached. The level of costs is determined by alternate opportunities for resource use. The question, "What is the marginal cost of producing steel?" cannot be determined unless we know (1) what is the intensity of need for steel and (2) what are the alternate uses for the factors engaged in steel making. To perform meaningful calculations, the price system must be linked with the decision-making system. Such a linkage is advocated by a small group of economists, including Kantorovich in the Soviet Union and Drewnowski in Poland.[12] In practice, the opposite course is taken. Since the primary role given to factory prices is the control of enterprise performance, factory prices are consciously isolated from demand and linked to the production side only.

The contrast between economic efficiency calculations and political considerations should not be drawn too strongly. After all, the policy makers' preferences take into account the availability of productive factors. The scarcity relations are also taken into account in the process of long-term and short-term planning. What is asserted here is that the possibility of economic calculus and the significance of such calculus in a soviet-type system is strictly limited:

[11] See, for instance, *Spór o ceny*, Warszawa, Książka i Wiedza, 1958.

[12] See Jan Drewnowski, "The Economic Theory of Socialism: A Suggestion for Reconsideration," *The Journal of Political Economy*, vol. 69, no. 4, August, 1961.

In a capitalist society the objective market valuation is a necessary prerequisite for economic calculus. Under socialism this objective method of appraisal had to be severely modified. As a consequence of the modification and limitation of this method of appraisal, numerous difficulties arose in the socialist system. Perhaps the greatest difficulties are connected with an objective and rapid appraisal of the rationality of the functioning of the investment goods sector.[13]

To perform meaningful calculations, the government may fix either quantities or prices, but not both. By resorting to direct administrative action in all the phases of economic life and by fixing prices and quantities, the leaders in the Soviet-bloc countries deprive themselves of the possibility of an over-all appraisal of results. The economy is fully planned, but resource allocation is virtually haphazard.

One can justly claim that waste is an inevitable by-product of investment regardless of the economic system. Investments are made to satisfy future needs which can never be exactly known in advance. In a market economy in which prices are reasonably close to opportunity cost, it is easier to perform investment efficiency calculations than in a soviet-type system. On the other hand the market merely predicts the future, while the Soviet policy makers plan the future. Planning reduces uncertainty, hence—one might surmise—it eliminates many investment errors. A defender of the soviet-type system might therefore claim that planning on the whole increases investment efficiency instead of decreasing it.

The argument that planning reduces investment waste hinges upon the specificity of the wishes of the political

[13] J. Popiel, "Pieniądz w gospodarce socjalistycznej," *Narodowy Bank Polski, Wiadomości*, vol. 15, no. 10, p. 481, 1959.

leadership. If the wishes are specific, events cannot prove the leadership to be wrong; no investment can be misdirected. Imagine, for instance, that the technology of nonferrous metals and of plastics advances rapidly and that the need for steel declines. Will the current drive to expand steel production turn out to be misdirected? If the leadership wants to build steel mills for the sake of having steel mills, the relative cost of production of steel and steel substitutes is irrelevant. If, on the other hand, the leadership wants steel capacity in order to maximize at some future date the output of products made with steel, the current drive might well involve resource waste. Thus, if the wishes are nonspecific, the question of superior rationality of investment under planning is reduced to the question of the foresight of planners as compared with the foresight of investors in a market system.

A comparison of the decision-making process followed by American businessmen and by Soviet administrators shows striking similarities. In both systems the elaborate calculations advocated by theorists are rarely if ever applied in practice; instead, there is a reliance on rules of thumb and on "business sense." Abstracting from the relative virtues of the data on which decisions are made, one may advance the tentative hypothesis that there is no great difference in the rationality of decision making under the two systems.

The fundamental difference lies in the error-correcting mechanism. An error committed by an enterprise in a market environment is reflected in the enterprise's profits. If the error is too great, the enterprise may be forced out of business. Monopolies and cartelization blunt the error-correcting instrument, but do not eliminate it. A monopolized steel industry competes with nonferrous metals. A cartelized air transport industry has to reckon with rail and road transport. Cartelization and monopolization do not punish errors as swiftly and as severely as competition, but the corrective mechanism is still present.

Soviet-type economies have done away with the automatism of error correction. To match the efficiency of market economies, they would have to perform infinitely more exact calculations. Yet the basic structure of the system denies the possibility of such calculations. Prices are deprived of any allocative role, and they are only a dim indicator for decision making. Plans are fitted together like a jig-saw puzzle. An individual piece cannot be trimmed or replaced without spoiling the whole picture unless all the pieces are changed as well:

> Each element of the plan enters a separate material balance. Although all elements are expressed in monetary terms, every one is irreplaceable without a central decision.[14]

Since the system of planning is rigid, the entire economy requires frequent overhauls. A weakness is tolerated as long as possible in order to avoid rearrangement of all the pieces. Finally, when the situation becomes unbearable, radical steps are taken to remedy it. Thus the economy proceeds by starts and jolts, with successive drives or campaigns to eliminate this or that mistake. At one time it may be excessive employment, at another it may be poor quality of product or lack of technical progress.

Partisans of soviet-type planning claim great virtues for the method of concentrated drives. Rather than disperse its

[14] W. Brus, *op. cit.*, p. 139.

energies in a myriad of directions, the nation focuses its forces on points which most urgently need reform. Hurdles are overcome one by one, and rapid and easily seen results are achieved.

The concentration of a nation's energies on a few urgent tasks has undeniable virtues. On the other hand, it must be noted that in soviet-type economies such urgent tasks constantly arise because the system has no way of coping with small everyday problems. Such problems accumulate over time, until waste becomes intolerable; if they could be adjusted as a part of the normal functioning of the economy, there would be no need to mobilize the nation's energies to cope with them.

The leadership in the soviet-type economies is deeply concerned about visible waste. Much thought and energy goes into the improvement of flow-coordination to prevent surpluses and shortages. Enterprises are rewarded for good performance and punished for poor results. Periodic drives are undertaken to improve the quality of products, to increase the productivity of labor, and to lessen the amount of raw materials utilized.

The efforts to eliminate visible waste do not touch on the fundamental problem of resource allocation. If visible waste is eradicated, a soviet-type economy might give an outward appearance of complete efficiency. There would be no bottlenecks, no delays, no accumulation of unnecessary inventories. The solution would then be perfectly consistent, yet it might involve very poor resource use from the point of view of the leadership. To make good use of resources, to use one example, it is not sufficient to balance the energy needs with the energy output. It is also necessary to calculate which source of energy to use to what extent, and how to allocate energy among diverse uses. The soviet-type economies are potentially able to make a perfect balance; however, they have no mechanism for rational determination of resource use and no mechanism for detecting and correcting errors.

Twenty-five years ago Oscar Lange laid the ghost of the theory that rational calculus is impossible in a socialist economy.[15] Even earlier the Soviet Union confounded its critics and ill-wishers by refusing to collapse through sheer waste. The two proofs are sometimes confused and the conclusion is drawn that soviet-type systems are rational and efficient.

Socialism, defined as the national ownership of all means of production, is compatible with a variety of institutional arrangements, some of which permit the use of economic calculus and lead to rational resource use. The soviet-type systems, defined as the institutional systems in force in the Soviet Union and in the other countries of the Soviet camp, are incapable of making such calculations. It does not follow that the soviet-type economies will collapse. A soviet-type economy enjoys almost absolute monopoly on all production within its political sphere, and there is no reason to question its survival powers. We cannot even conclude that the free world will outproduce the soviet-type economies or "win the economic race." The functioning of the free-market economies is far from perfect, and the aims of the two systems are entirely different. The free-market economies strive to satisfy the needs revealed by the market. In the

[15] See Oscar Lange, "On the Economic Theory of Socialism," in B. Lipincott (ed.), *On the Economic Theory of Socialism*, Minneapolis, The University of Minnesota Press, 1938.

Soviet-bloc countries the leadership is willing to disregard present needs and build for the future. Even if the process is more wasteful, it may result in faster growth than the market process.

Ultimately, perhaps even in the not-too-distant future, soviet-type economies might produce more consumer goods than free-enterprise nations. They will have won the "economic race," but the victory will not be a proof of their superiority. The "victory" will show that one can achieve rapid results if one is willing to make sufficiently great sacrifices. Whether the sacrifices demanded by the soviet-type systems from their citizens are warranted in terms of the results is an ethical question, and not one of scientific judgment.

Index